BARRON'S BUSINESS LIBRARY

Accounting and Taxation

BARRON'S BUSINESS LIBRARY

Accounting and Taxation

Walter F. O'Connor
Fordham Graduate School of Business

New York • London • Toronto • Sydney

All inquiries should be addressed to:
Barron's Educational Series, Inc.
250 Wireless Boulevard
Hauppauge, New York 11788

Library of Congress Catalog Card Number 89-18305

International Standard Book Number 0-8120-4154-2

Library of Congress Cataloging-in-Publication Data

O'Connor, Walter F.
   Accounting and taxation / by Walter F. O'Connor.
      p. cm. — (Barron's business library)
   ISBN 0-8120-4154-2
   1. Financial statements. 2. Accounting. 3. Business enterprises—
Taxation—United States. I. Title. II. Series.
HF5681.B2027 1990
657'.46—dc20   89-18305
                                          CIP

PRINTED IN ITALY

Foreword

This book is not only a step-by-step guide to the field of accounting as it relates to the operations of a business enterprise, it is also a ready reference that managers and owners can keep on their desks, ready to help them solve problems as they occur.

From the first chapter, Why Accounting?, on through explanations of assets and liabilities, income and costs, budgets and profit centers, managerial accounting and financial accounting, the focus is always on the business as it exists in the real world. Theories and general principles are discussed in terms of their practical applications. To this end there are numerous examples of financial reports—income statements, balance sheets, budgets, etc.—to illustrate the points being made in the text. There are also incisive discussions of such important matters as managerial accounting, flexible budgeting, and other tools to use in coping with today's competitive business environment. And throughout, explanations are given in light of the tax consequences of each decision.

In sum, this book gives business managers and owners valuable insights into the often complex world of accounting.

THE EDITORS

Contents

BARRON'S BUSINESS LIBRARY

Accounting and Taxation

Why Accounting?

INTRODUCTION AND MAIN POINTS

In this chapter we will give you an understanding of the reasons why accounting and taxation are important to each person in business. As the "language" of business, accounting and taxation impact all areas of business from the most simple activity to the most sophisticated. In this chapter we will concentrate on why accounting is important and what kind of businesspeople need accounting information. In this way we will lay the foundation for people who have little knowledge of the subject to begin to understand not only what accounting is, but why it will help them in their business lives on a day-to-day basis. This chapter will also give you a feeling of how accounting and taxation interrelate in the business world.

After studying the material in this chapter;

▬ You will see what types of businesspeople require accounting information.

▬ You will understand the differences between financial accounting, managerial accounting, and taxation accounting and how they relate to one another.

▬ You will begin to understand the role played by the various types of accountants and the types of accounting information with which they deal.

▬ You will understand the way in which accounting information is accumulated for business purposes and usages.

▬ You will be exposed to the standards that are used in assembling accounting information.

▬ You will develop an initial feeling for the types of financial statements that will be discussed in greater detail in this book.

Many books on accounting and taxation delve into this subject from the standpoint of the writer instead of the reader. That is, they assume certain understanding of the subject of accounting on the part of the reader, then proceed to discuss those matters with which it is assumed the reader is familiar. This, however, begins the journey in the middle of the stream. But for our purposes, let us start at the very beginning: Why should we have accounting at all?

A second starting vantage point is the crossing between financial accounting, managerial accounting, and taxation (subjects to be explained later) without showing the reader the interrelation of these three areas. At this point, let's just say that:

▬ Financial accounting deals with information primarily of value to people outside the business.

▬ Managerial accounting is used by people running the business.

▬ Taxation accounting deals with the rules needed to determine the taxable income to be reported to tax authorities.

Once again, books delve into the subjects as if they were separate and apart from each other. However, in the real world business executives are dealing with financial accounting, managerial accounting, and taxation accounting on an interchangeable basis. This is because they approach the whole subject from a business transaction standpoint.

It is assumed that the reader of this book is primarily interested in the subject in order to answer the question, "Given the fact that I have business decisions facing me, what do I have to know about accounting and taxation?" This approach will be the focal point of this book. For that reason, let's take a look at some fundamental issues regarding accounting and taxation in a nontraditional way. What we will do is cut across the lines of financial accounting, managerial accounting, and tax accounting and see how particular business issues are viewed from different accounting standpoints.

WHAT IS ACCOUNTING?

While there are as many definitions of accounting as there are accountants, we need a practical definition. Let us say that accounting is the identification, measurement, and communication of financial information about business entities to be used by interested persons. This definition takes into consideration the fact that accounting is a discipline that has value since parties that are involved with particular businesses need quantitative information (numbers) about that business in order to make their evaluations.

These evaluations could be those of suppliers to the business, customers of the business, employees of the business, investors in the business, government agencies to which the business is responsible in one way or the other, and finally (but not the least) the owners of the business itself.

An additional aspect of accounting is its ability to enable the interested parties to make business decisions based on the information received. Consequently, accounting is not a static discipline but rather one that should provide the users of the information the means whereby they are able to make intelligent business decisions.

WHO IS INTERESTED IN ACCOUNTING INFORMATION?

From a financial accounting standpoint, people outside the business entity would be the ones primarily interested in financial information. For example, potential stockholders, banks and other financial institutions, people selling goods and services to the business entity, and customers would all be interested parties outside the business entity.

From the standpoint of managerial accounting, the main focus is on accounting information for use by people inside the company, including the chief executive officer, chief financial officer, operating division heads, department chiefs, the controller—in short, all those who are involved with running the business from a marketing, production, research, and financial standpoint. Now, that is a significant number of people to be depending on accounting information in order to run the business. As we will see later, this puts a high value on creating a system that records transactions only one time but makes that information part of a system so that it is available for multipurpose usages for the benefit of the business.

From a tax standpoint, accounting information is needed with regard to the planning of future events (in that context, dealing with projections of future income and expenses) as well as to the defense of the positions taken by the taxpayers when challenged by government agencies such as the Internal Revenue Service and the state and local tax jurisdictions. The tax issue is a tricky one in that the tax laws themselves prescribe rules for accounting for transactions, and these rules often differ from the standards involved in financial and managerial accounting. Here again, however, the initial input of accounting information for transactions would be the starting point for bringing the information into the tax discipline for compliance and planning purposes.

WHO NEEDS ACCOUNTING INFORMATION?

From a financial accounting standpoint, businesspeople require accounting information to prepare a "report card" for the various parties outside the business having relevant interests. For example, shareholders are interested in information that tells them how their company has done during some period of time in the past as well as what the status of the company is, as of a given date. For these purposes, the traditional income statement and balance sheet are the two documents that provide people outside the company with the information they need. We will see that accounting standards do not always provide the type of information that will enable a person to readily ascertain the fair market value of a share of stock on a particular date, because of the financial accounting standard reliance on historical costs for reflecting certain figures. However, to governmental agencies such as the Securities and Exchange Commission, the traditional reports provide information based on a wealth of historical standards, which provide consistency to the reporting of information—an essential for the readers. (The Securities and Exchange Commission (SEC) is a Federal agency that has the responsibility and authority for regulating the accounting profession as it relates to information on companies whose securities are offered to the general public in the United States.)

From a managerial accounting standpoint, the people inside the company need accounting information in order to keep the score card with regard to how the company is doing. This card begins with the setting of budgets for the future activity of a division or department, then is carried through to (and includes) the ultimate measurement of actual performance against such budgets to determine how the subsections of the company are doing.

From the standpoint of tax accounting, the Internal Revenue Service and other government entities need the information in order to determine the tax liability of the business. The tax return is another type of score card with regard to how the company has done.

From the standpoint of the company itself, the tax personnel need accounting information in order to engage in the planning of future transactions as well as the filing of tax returns that are required for reporting to the governmental agencies.

WHEN DOES ACCOUNTING INFORMATION HAVE TO BE PRODUCED?

There is a wide divergence of timings with regard to the production of accounting information because of the needs of the various parties for the information.

From a financial accounting standpoint, the requirement of quarterly information for larger companies is created by the Securities and Exchange Commission as well as other government agencies who make this a prerequisite for the registration of financial instruments to be acceptable. Indeed in the recent past, management has been criticized in some quarters for being too short-term oriented, focusing too much on the quarterly earnings statement. However, given the requirement placed on business by outside governmental agencies, it is easy to see why a focus of this type is important. Indeed, the shareholders themselves are partly responsible for the short-term element of financial accounting because of the importance they place on such statements in their evaluations of the success of the management of the company.

To place this short-term information in perspective, financial accounting also involves information on long-term trends. For example, many public companies will have five- and ten-year or even longer periods reflected in the annual report to shareholders in order to give a feeling of the strategies that have been adopted and how they have been implemented. This score card then indicates the importance of accounting information on a long-term basis as well as a short-term basis.

From a managerial accounting standpoint, accounting information is generally required and produced on more frequent time frames. "Flash reports" by department heads will often involve the production of key figures on a monthly, weekly, or even daily basis in order to keep a constant watch on how things are working in the company from an accounting standpoint. (A flash report is terminology used by companies for information that is prepared and communicated quickly to give management some idea as to whether their plans are moving along in accordance with their expectations.) Information at these frequent intervals enables the company to make mid-course corrections during an operating period. Management can thus make changes in a way that produces the minimum number of surprises at the end of a reporting period to outsiders relying on the financial accounting information system.

From a tax accounting standpoint, time frames also vary. For example, taxpayers are required to file annual tax returns and self-assess their tax position with the Internal Revenue Service. Because of the cash flow needs of government, it has become routine to require that tax payments be made during the taxable year based on estimates of what the ultimate liability will be. (Self-assessment means that under the United States tax law we, as taxpayers, compute our own tax liability and report that to the government.) Such estimates require quarterly tax payments to be made, thus creating a need for quarterly tax accounting information.

WHO IS INVOLVED IN PREPARING ACCOUNTING INFORMATION?

The people involved in preparing financial accounting information are both inside and outside the company. The financial statements that go to outside parties are the responsibility of the company itself. Consequently, the accounting department of the company will be primarily involved in the assemblage of the information. However, the credibility of the information gains strength by having it reviewed by independent outside parties. This is the role of the Certified Public Accountant (CPA). In developing the audit reviews of a company's information, the CPA is able to ascertain whether a company's financial statements have been produced in accordance with accounting standards that have become generally accepted over the years. While the independent CPA does not find all mistakes that might be made in financial statements, he or she is able to determine whether the financial statements are fairly presented in a way that will give the reader some assurance that no material misstatements are involved. Once having made such a determination, the CPA will very often produce a report somewhat similar to the one reproduced on the next page.

From a managerial accounting standpoint, the internal accounting system takes over in the production of information needed by various subunits of the company. They can be people either at a centralized location or people spread throughout operating divisions of the business enterprise. There is a parallel here with regard to the CPA for financial information in that most companies of any size have an internal audit unit department that works within the organization to determine that information

REPORT OF
INDEPENDENT CERTIFIED PUBLIC ACCOUNTANTS

TO THE STOCKHOLDERS AND
BOARD OF DIRECTORS OF JOHNSON & JOHNSON:

We have examined the consolidated balance sheet of Johnson & Johnson and subsidiaries as of December 28, 1986 and December 29, 1985, and the related consolidated statements of earnings and retained earnings, common stock, additional capital and treasury stock, and cash flows for each of the three years in the period ended December 28, 1986. Our examinations were made in accordance with generally accepted auditing standards and, accordingly, included such tests of the accounting records and such other auditing procedures as we considered necessary in the circumstances.

In our opinion, the financial statements referred to above present fairly the financial position of Johnson & Johnson and subsidiaries at December 28, 1986 and December 29, 1985, and the results of their operations and the changes in their financial position for each of the three years in the period ended December 28, 1986, in conformity with generally accepted accounting principles applied on a consistent basis.

New York, New York
February 11, 1987

This reporting format has been fairly standardized since the 1940s. In recent years demand has been placed on the accounting profession to do more in the area of fraud detection.[1] The result of this has been a study whose results were released in 1987. As a result of that study, the Treadway Report[2] was issued, requiring the CPA to utilize a new form of opinion that looks as follows:

NEW REPORT OF CERTIFIED PUBLIC ACCOUNTANTS

We have studied the accompanying balance sheets of X Company as of December 31, 1989 and 1988, and the related statements of income, retained earnings, and cash flows for the years then ended. These financial statements are the responsibility of the Company's management. Our responsibility is to express an opinion on these financial statements based on our audits.

We conducted our audits in accordance with generally accepted auditing standards. Those standards require that we plan and perform the audit to obtain reasonable assurance about whether the financial statements are free of material misstatement. An audit includes examining, on a test basis evidence supporting the amounts and disclosures in the financial statements. An audit also includes assessing the accounting principles used and significant estimates made by management, as well as evaluating the overall financial statement presentation. We believe that our audits provide a reasonable basis for our opinion.

In our opinion, the financial statements referred to above present fairly, in all material respects, the financial position of X Company as of (at) December 31, 1989 and 1988, and the results of its operations and its cash flow for the years then ended in conformity with generally accepted accounting principles.

(Signature)
(Date)

[Optional paragraph if company is in financial trouble:]
The accompanying financial statements have been prepared assuming that Company Y will continue as a going concern. As discussed in Note X to the financial statements, Company Y has suffered recurring losses from operations and has a net capital deficiency that raises substantial doubt about the entity's ability to continue as a going concern. Management's plans in regard to these matters are also described in Note X. The financial statements do not include any adjustments that might result from the outcome of this uncertainty.

being produced is reliable and also enables the company to have assurance that internal reports have credibility. This is an important function in any organization, given the fact that the operating divisions produce the accounting information that is used to measure the performance of those divisions. If an internal audit function did not exist, this information could be manipulated to give a false picture of a division's performance.

With regard to managerial accounting, a profession has developed, that of Certified Management Accountants (CMA). These are distinguished from CPAs in that their job is to focus on internal accounting information, which is different from that used for reporting to outside parties. Just as the CPA fraternity has as its mother organization, the American Institute of Certified Public Accountants, the National Association of Accountants is involved with the CMA qualification. Given the manner in which American businesses have been criticized in comparison with businesses in other countries, such as Japan, for not performing as well, the CMA accreditation is one that is gaining in importance in the American economy.

The people involved with tax accounting information are the tax departments of companies and, on the outside, the Internal Revenue Service. The tax function in many companies involves people engaged in strategic planning; in negotiation with legislators as well as with Treasury Department officials, trying to get rules changed or clarified; in dealing with the Internal Revenue agents auditing the tax returns of taxpayers; as well as in accumulating the information to be put on the tax forms to be filed with the government agencies.

Finally, regarding the matter of who is involved, one of the difficulties that arise in business is the lack of communication between operating people and people needing financial and tax information. It seems to be axiomatic that the better communication there is among these various parties, the better is the quality of the accounting and tax information produced as well as the more efficient is the utilization of that information throughout the organization.

HOW IS ACCOUNTING INFORMATION REFLECTED?

Financial accounting information is assembled by recording quantitative information about transactions that take place during the course of the life of the business. The so-called double-entry system was created centuries ago and has been adopted by most cases, from the simplest one-person operation to the most complex multinational corporation. (The double-entry system refers to the mechanism by which, when a business transaction is entered into, for each record of the transaction there is an offsetting item that enables the company to keep control of the recording of the transaction. To put it more simply, if a sale is made for cash, the recording of the sale is offset by a recording of the cash. Thus at any time, there is a way of cross checking to make sure an entry has been recorded properly.) Computerization has made these transactions move at much higher speed, but the basics are still more or less the same. Consequently, the "how" of accounting information begins at the recording of a single transaction using such a double-entry system. Checks and balances with regard to the inputting of such information and the extraction of meaningful reports from it all form part of the system used to provide the people outside the company with the information in which they are interested.

From a managerial accounting standpoint, the budgeting process (as a starting point in many instances) also starts with the basic raw material of a double-entry accounting system. The saying "the past is prologue" could not be truer in this area, since very few budgets start without relying in some way on historical information being captured in a company's internal accounting system. The sales journals, purchase journals, cash receipts and disbursements journals, trial balances, adjusting entries, general ledgers, and closing entries are part of the jargon that goes with the details of an accounting system. (The term *journal* refers to a record in accounting that lists a series of similar transactions, e.g., sales or purchases. The term *ledger* refers to an accounting record that accumulates in one place information dealing with a series of different types of transactions that would have been accumulated in journals.)

Is it essential for the businessperson reading this book to delve into the minutia that goes with the mechanics of such a system? No. Suffice it to say, however, that unless the accounting system is constructed in a manner that will detect errors on a going-forward basis, the foundation of the company's financial accounting as well as its managerial accounting will be faulty. An automobile parts manufacturer in the United States used to run an advertisement on television with the slogan "You can pay me now or pay me later." The idea of the commercial was that if you didn't buy a five dollar oil filter now to protect the engine, you would have to pay several hundred dollars later to repair a damaged motor. The accounting system of a business is equivalent in the sense that a faulty system will produce results that can misguide and mislead business executives and their many publics.

A tax accounting system is generally run on two levels. First it involves the filing of forms with the government authorities to report the transactions. Secondly, it involves the auditing of those figures by government authorities to check on the credibility of the taxpayer's returns. Here again, the raw material comes from the internal accounting system of the company, although adjustments often have to be made to that information to convert accounting and managerial accounting information to what is required by the tax laws at the federal, state, or local level.

WHAT IS THE PROCESS FOR ACCUMULATING ACCOUNTING INFORMATION?

For financial accounting purposes, there is what is known as an accounting cycle, which traces the recording of information from the time the transaction is entered into to the use of that information in published financial statements. Figure 1-1 gives in a schematic form what that cycle looks like.

As you can see, the process starts with the identification and quantification of a transaction. For example, the purchase of inventory would involve the recording of the asset acquired (inventory) and the liability incurred (accounts payable) to reflect that transaction. After a number of such transactions have been accumulated for the required period of time over which the information is to be measured, they are summarized in a form called a trial balance. Such a trial balance summarizes the assets, liabilities, income, and expense that are impacted by such transactions as recorded. Since many transactions involve accounting information that is not produced by a specific transaction, adjustments also have to be made to the trial balance. For example, if a company prepays its rental expense for a three-year period of time, it would be inappropriate to impact a one-year period of income with three years of rental expense. Consequently, an adjustment would be made to reflect part of that payment as a current expense and another part as an asset to be allocated over the relevant future periods. (The term *adjustment* means an alteration of the accounts after all transactions have been recorded. These alterations are made in order to take into account a proper matching of income and expense where the original recording of the transaction did not properly do so.) Adjustments of this type for prepaid expenses and accrued liabilities are common in the accounting cycle.

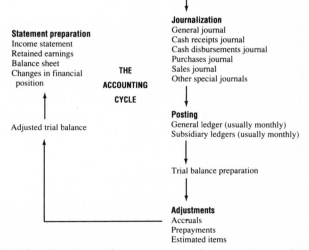

FIG. 1-1 *Identification and measurement of transactions and other events*

Once all adjustments are made, the process then moves on to creating a final trial balance. This document provides the basis for the formulation of an income statement of the results of the current period, a statement of change in the equity (owner's accounts in the business), and also a balance sheet that provides a statement of financial condition as of a given date. This process takes place at the time of "the closing" of the accounts of a business. Such a closing involves the assemblage of information, which in effect is the report card for the company for a time period and as of a given date.

From a managerial accounting standpoint, the process is geared primarily to measuring actual results against budgeted figures. The budget could involve the anticipation of how a division will record income and expenses in the future, what the expectations are with regard to the purchasing of inventory, selling it, and collecting accounts receivable, or the outlook for more long-term projects such as capital expenditures for machinery and equipment or indeed even entire businesses. There is a similarity between managerial and financial accounting in that the process involves the accumulation of actual data and then producing results that enable people (either outside or inside the company) to make evaluations about performance.

With regard to tax accounting, the process generally involves the accumulation of information from the accounting system in general and adjusting it to the requirements of the Internal Revenue Code and other legislation. In situations where the tax filings are not challenged by the tax authorities, the process generally ends with the completion and filing of tax returns in accordance with laws prescribed. This is often a tedious process for companies since there are many differences between financial accounting and managerial accounting on the one hand and tax accounting on the other hand. For example, companies will very often have different methods of depreciating their fixed assets for tax purposes and for accounting purposes. A company can decide to take advantage of accelerated methods of depreciation, which permit the taxpayer to write off assets in a tax-deductible way, in order to reduce tax liability at an early stage of the ownership of the equipment, whereas it can adopt other methods for financial statement and managerial accounting purposes. (Accelerated methods of depreciation mean the recording of a depreciation expense that writes off larger amounts in the early part of the life of the asset than would take place if the expense were recorded by an equal amount each year.) A key point here is that there need not be conformity between the manner in which methods are used for tax and the manner used for other accounting purposes. This does not mean that one system is "right" and the other "wrong" but rather that there are different methods available for different purposes, one being the reflection of financial and managerial accounting results and the other being a reduction of tax liability to the maximum legitimate degree.

WHAT IS MEANT BY INTERNAL CONTROL IN AN ACCOUNTING SYSTEM?

For financial accounting purposes, internal control connotes the system set up within the company to assure, to the extent possible, that the information produced is as credible as possible. Without internal control, a company could never be sure that the information it produces is reliable enough to use to make decisions or to report results. Internal control is a subject all to itself. Suffice it to say at this point that it is the system of checks and balances put into the recording of accounting information that ensures that the end results produced will be as trustworthy as possible. It is a key factor for financial accounting in that the audits by independent CPAs rely very heavily on a company's internal-control system in determining the extent to which detailed checking has to be done to assure reliability. In cases where the internal-control system is strong, the CPA needs do less checking (and consequently the audit is less expensive). On the other hand, where the controls are weak, it can range to a point where a CPA will decide that the company cannot even be audited.

From a managerial accounting standpoint, internal control has the same objective, namely to assure the reliability of the accounting information. Internal auditors will very often provide the function that independent CPAs provide for financial accounting—evaluating the system and relying on it in formulating an audit plan. They will review the way in which systems are set up and also the way in which such systems are adhered to in practice. Good internal control on paper that is not implemented is worthless!

From a tax accounting standpoint, internal control means that the results put on tax returns have a high degree of reliability and, as a result, there are reasonable assurances that, when a tax return is audited by a governmental authority, it will withstand the scrutiny from the standpoint of credibility. Where tax authorities find that the accounting system lacks strong internal controls, they will legitimately question whether the filings by the taxpayer can be relied upon.

BY WHAT STANDARDS IS ACCOUNTING INFORMATION MEASURED?

From a financial accounting standpoint, the term "Generally Accepted Accounting Principles" (GAAP) is key to the reliability of the system. Without GAAP, companies could record the same transactions in widely divergent ways, thus leaving the reader of the financial statement with no good feeling for the manner in which company results can be evaluated. We will discuss a little later in detail what GAAP means for various types of accounting transactions. At this point, however, you can see GAAP as the ground rules under which companies are required to operate in order to make sure that there is as much comparability of financial information among companies and also within a company from year to year.

From a managerial accounting standpoint, the measurement system for accounting information must closely relate to the cost-benefit relationship of accumulating that information. While it is generally very desirable to have available a lot of information, we are quickly reaching a point (because of the advent of the computer) of "information overload." For example, in analyzing the operation of a division, a listing of all the accounts receivable would not be as meaningful as an analysis aging the accounts receivable by the period of time they are outstanding. The receivables that continually get older and older tell management that there may be danger points in the running of that part of the business, whereas a raw listing of all the receivables would be meaningless.

The GAAP standards for financial accounting find their way into managerial accounting, however, and the two should not be considered separate standards for measuring transactions. It may well be, however, that for internal purposes, revenues and expenses or assets and liabilities might be classified in different ways in order to produce more meaningful results for subsections of the company. For example, from a managerial accounting standpoint, cash flow may be a more important criterion for certain measurements than GAAP, which relies more heavily on accrual-basis reporting. As a result, the measurement of the relationship of collecting receivables and accounting for payables can be more important for managerial accounting than for financial accounting at a particular time.

From a tax accounting standpoint, the measurement system is basically the Internal Revenue Code or other legislation that impacts the recording of business transactions. As mentioned earlier, there are differences between GAAP and the Internal Revenue Code, and properly so. This difference in the types of the rules and the transactions to which they apply has to be taken into account in the business of any company.

WHAT ARE THE END RESULT STATEMENTS PRODUCED BY ACCOUNTING INFORMATION?

By this time the answer to this question should be fairly obvious.

For financial statements purposes, the income statement, balance sheet, statement of changes in ownership, and (in more recent years) statement of changes in working capital (or cash flow) are the primary results of a financial accounting system.

A managerial accounting system, on the other hand, is focused more on accounting information for subsections of the company as a whole, thus is directed to the production of budgets for future activity and to a measurement of actual results for comparison with budgets for performance measurement. In addition, ratio analysis is important in the managerial accounting area. Such ratios as advertising expense to total sales, turnover of inventory, lock up of investment in accounts receivable, and research and development expenditures to total cost are very often critical factors in a managerial accounting system evaluation. (The term "turnover," when related to inventory, means the speed with which a business can acquire or produce inventory for sale, sell it, and collect the cash on it. The quicker this can be done, the less the business is investing in inventory and the quicker it is earning profits. The term "lock up" means the amount of time that your customer has the use of your money by virtue of you having an account receivable from that customer. It is the extent to which you are playing banker for your customer.)

From a tax accounting standpoint, a final statement produced would be the tax forms that are filed by taxpayers with the governmental agencies. Such forms are structured to reflect the income and expense of an enterprise in such a way as to enable tax authorities to determine the fair tax liability of the entity. Given the fact that tax laws change frequently, the changes in the forms and the information to be put on those forms has to be continually under review in order to make certain that taxpayers do not overpay their liability but pay their fair share as legislators intended.

Given this overview of how accounting information varies or whether it is used for financial, managerial, or tax purposes, we are now in a position to take a look at what makes up the end results of these accounting systems and how the financial, managerial, and tax aspects interrelate.

CHAPTER PERSPECTIVE

In this chapter we have begun the process of exposing you as a businessperson to the rudiments of accounting and taxation. Assuming you knew nothing about the subject prior to reading this chapter, you now have a foundation based on looking at the big picture. You have an appreciation of why accounting is needed as well as who is involved in accumulating that information.

You have also had a chance to see, in a preliminary way, what information is produced for people outside the company as well as for internal management. Of additional value at this stage is your preliminary understanding of the accounting cycle, which reflects how the business transactions work their way into being recorded. Ultimately, these records lead to the creation of financial statements that can be utilized in different ways to measure the performance of a business.

You also have gained an appreciation for the fact that there are uniform standards for recording accounting transactions so that, in the future, you will be able to compare your company's activities with prior periods as well as with your competitor's activities.

This chapter has given us the basis for looking in greater depth into individual elements of accounting information. We will now begin in Chapter 2 to look at those elements in more detail.

FOOTNOTES

1 *Statement on Auditing Standards No. 53 The Auditor's Responsibility to Detect and Report Errors and Irregularities. (American Institute of Certified Public Accountants.)*

2 *Report of the National Commission on Fraudulent Financial Reporting (October, 1987).*

The Resources of the Business Enterprise

INTRODUCTION AND MAIN POINTS

In this chapter we will expand your understanding of the accounting and taxation rules as they relate to the part of the company resources that generate income. Specifically, we will examine what are called the assets of the company so that you gain an appreciation of the manner in which they are accounted for in the financial statements.

After studying the material in this chapter:

■ You will have a feeling for the various kinds of assets owned by a company and the way in which accounting rules apply to them.

■ You will see what part of the balance sheet of a company the assets occupy and how the various kinds of assets are classified on that balance sheet.

■ You will develop a feeling for the time frame involved in the ownership of assets from the most liquid type of assets (e.g., cash) to the most long-term (e.g., buildings).

■ You will gain an appreciation of the limitations of the balance sheet as it relates to assets, owing to the interrelationship of historical costs and fair market value of the assets.

■ You will develop an understanding of the differences between the treatment of assets for tax purposes and their treatment for general accounting purposes.

The resources of a business are often described as "assets" and connote the wherewithal by which businesses are able to carry out their economic objectives. (By "asset" we mean an economic resource owned by a business that is expected to benefit future operations.) Assets are a main portion of a balance sheet, and for that reason the businessperson should have familiarity with the underlying principles used when this accounting information is recorded.

The assets are recorded on the balance sheet, which provides information at a particular date about the nature and amounts of investment in the resources of an enterprise, obligations to enterprise creditors, and the owner's equity in the net enterprise resources. This information not only complements information about the components of income, but also contributes to financial reporting by providing a basis for (1) computing rates of return, (2) evaluating the capital structure of the enterprise, and (3) assessing the liquidity and financial flexibility of the enterprise. In order to make certain judgments about enterprise risk and assessments of future cash flows, the businessperson must analyze the balance sheet and determine enterprise liquidity and financial flexibility.

LIQUIDITY AND FLEXIBILITY

Liquidity describes the amount of time that is expected to elapse until an asset is realized or otherwise converted into cash or until a liability has to be paid.[1] Both short-term and long-term credit grantors are interested in the relationship of such short-term measures as cash to current liabilities in order to assess the enterprise's ability to meet current and maturing obligations. Similarly, stockholders study the liquidity of an enterprise to assess the likelihood of continuing or increased cash dividends or the possibility of expanded operations. The greater the liquidity, the lower the risk of enterprise failure.

Financial flexibility, on the other hand, is the ability of an enterprise to take effective actions to alter the amounts and timing of cash flows so that it can respond to unexpected needs and opportunities.[2] For example, a company may become so burdened with debt that its sources of monies to finance expansion or to pay off maturing debt are limited or nonexistent. An enterprise with a high degree of financial flexibility is better able to survive bad times, to recover from unexpected setbacks, and to take advantage of profitable and unexpected investment opportunities. The greater the financial flexibility, the lower the risk of enterprise failure.

As an illustration, one need look no further than the experience of the airline industry in the United States. Pan Am, American, Eastern, United, and TWA all reported operating losses in the early 1980s that stemmed primarily from high interest rates, deregulation that increased competition, increased fuel costs, and price cutting. Because of operating losses and lowered liquidity, some airlines even asked their employees to sign labor contracts that provided no wage increases. Other airlines had to cancel orders for new, more efficient aircraft and were not even able to generate cash from the sale of their old aircraft because of lower air traffic and the lower fuel efficiency of the older aircraft. Airline balance sheets at that time revealed their financial inflexibility and low liquidity.

An illustration of more recent vintage would be the rash of leveraged buyouts (LBOs) in the late 1980s. Here borrowings in the billions of dollars put many companies in postures of significantly less flexibility. If business goes bad, the ability to service that debt could be sharply limited, resulting in a loss of flexibility.

LIMITATIONS OF THE BALANCE SHEET

But does the balance sheet give all the answers to all the readers? The answer is unequivocally No. The balance sheet does not reflect current value because accountants have adopted an historical cost basis in reporting the assets and liabilities. When a balance sheet is prepared in accordance with GAAP, most assets are stated at historical cost. For example, a property purchased in 1960 is still carried at its original price, without regard for the inflation in values that has occurred in the intervening years. Many accountants believe that all the assets should be restated in terms of current values; however, there are widely differing opinions about the exact type of valuation basis to be employed.

Another limitation of a balance sheet is that judgment must be exercised by the user. Even if significant changes in price levels do not occur, the determination of the collectability of receivables, the saleability of inventory, and the useful life of long-term tangible and intangible assets are difficult to determine.

In addition, the balance sheet necessarily omits many of the items that are of financial value to the business but cannot be recorded objectively. The value of a company's human resources is certainly significant, but it is omitted because such assets are difficult to quantify as a result of the uncertainty surrounding their ultimate value. Some companies say that a high percentage of their assets go down the elevator every night and come back in the morning.

Many items that could and should appear on the balance sheet are reported in an "off balance sheet" manner.[3] (By "off balance sheet" we mean a company resource that is not reflected on its financial statements. An example would be a valuable bit of technology whose costs were all expensed at the time they were incurred so that no item appears on the balance sheet related to that technology.)

Given these qualities and shortcomings, let us take a look at some of the more crucial assets that are reported on the balance sheet. A key classification differentiates assets between those that are current and those that are long-term. Current assets are cash and other assets that are expected to be converted into cash, sold, or consumed either in one year or in the operating cycle of the company, whichever is longer. For this purpose, the operating cycle of any given enterprise is considered to be the average time between the acquisition of materials and supplies and the realization of cash through sales of the product for which the materials and supplies were acquired.

From a financial accounting standpoint, these current assets are viewed as the short-term resources of the company; they are recorded according to GAAP rules. Cash is included at its stated value, marketable securities are valued at the cost or at lower of cost or market value, accounts receivable are stated at the estimated amount collectible, inventories generally are included at cost or the lower of cost or market, and prepaid items are valued at unexpired cost. ("Unexpired cost" means an expenditure that a company has made for an item that has a usefulness for more than one accounting period. An example would be a payment for insurance coverage for three years, which has a value to the company beyond the year in which the three-year premium is paid.)

At the very outset, it can, therefore, be seen that the conservatism of the accounting profession rears its head by making certain that such assets are recorded at current values only when those values are lower than cost. (The term "conservatism" is used frequently in accounting discussions. When accountants are faced with major uncertainties as to which alternative accounting procedure to apply, they tend to exercise caution and chose the procedure that is least likely to overstate assets or income.) If a company has a current asset whose value is greater than cost, that appreciation will not find its way into the results of the company until sometime in the future, when that asset is turned into cash.

From a managerial accounting standpoint, it might well be that departures from GAAP will be entered into and more emphasis will be placed on short-term assets of this type based on what their realizable value is at the current time. In situations where the fair market value is readily determinable, this may be a good approach to follow in order to give company management an opportunity of seeing what actually happened both in terms of depreciation and appreciation of assets during the period to be measured.

From a tax accounting standpoint, a major area of interest with regard to current assets is very often whether a taxpayer has taken deductions for depreciation of assets before they would be allowable for tax purposes. Tax rules very often follow the concept of completed transactions. Consequently they would not allow a taxpayer to take deductions merely because an asset has depreciated in value but yet has not been realized through a completed transaction (e.g., an actual sale). In recent years, the tax rules with regard to bad-debt allowances for accounts receivable are a good example. In the past, there was wide flexibility with regard to claiming bad-debt deductions, particularly for companies in the banking and insurance industries. But many of these flexibilities have been taken away, as the Internal Revenue Code has gone the direction of allowing bad debts only when actually incurred.

MARKETABLE SECURITIES

With regard to current assets such as marketable securities, financial accounting requires that they be valued at cost or the lower of cost or market value. What this means is that, by and large, where a marketable security has depreciated in value, that paper loss will be reflected in the financial statements for the current period. However, it should be noted that if that security appreciates in value, the accounting convention would not permit the reporting company to reflect that gain. This is an area in which businesspeople shake their heads at accounting standards, trying to see consistency in a practice of this type. The basic answer is that conservatism in the accounting profession takes over and dictates this type of rule.

From a managerial accounting standpoint, these standards may be different. For example, if a division of a company has sold some equipment and has the utilization of the funds for a short period of time, they will very often invest those in short-term marketable securities so that their funds do not lay idle. It would seem reasonable at that point for the appreciation resulting from those securities to be reflected in the division's results. Admittedly, the operating division is not in the business of short-term investing (a fact of which the treasurer in the organization will often remind the division). However, this would be considered part of the overall operations of that division. This point may be more academic than practical in the sense that the financial function of many corporations regularly "sweeps" divisions of excess cash so that those funds can be invested at a centralized level. (By "sweeping" cash is meant the treasury function of a company extracting cash that accumulates in operating divisions and departments so that it can be pulled together and invested in a manner that gives the company the greatest rate of return.)

With regard to the tax area, the financial accounting standard of lower of cost or market would not be permitted to result in the taxpayer taking a tax deduction for a depreciation in value of securities that have not yet been sold. This would, therefore, be an area in which information gathering for tax purposes would have to be structured in such a way as to permit the adjustment of financial accounting figures to avoid their being used improperly for tax purposes.

INVENTORIES

Inventories are a major current asset of many businesses. For financial accounting purposes, they are very often carried at cost or the lower of cost or market. (In connection with inventory methods, the term "market" does not refer to the fair market value or sales price of the item but rather the cost at which it can be replaced by the company either through purchase or through manufacturing.) Thus, where it would cost less to reacquire or reproduce inventories than what it originally cost the company to purchase or make them, this lower amount would be reflected in the financial accounting figures.

Inventories present a confusing subject because even the determination of cost can be done under various methods. You would think that what an item cost is what it should be recorded at. However, with companies acquiring hundreds, thousands, and sometimes millions of items of inventory, it is not realistic to try to identify a particular cost of a particular item every time one item is sold from the inventory. Consequently, two main methods have emerged as the ones most likely to be used, the Weighted Average Cost method and the First In/First Out (FIFO) methods. The first method determines cost by dividing the total cost of all purchases by the number of units of inventory.

The FIFO method works on the assumption that the first item acquired is the first item that is sold; consequently, it is the latest items purchased that remain in the inventory at the end of an accounting period.

Some readers may wonder why we did not list the Last In/First Out (LIFO) method as one of the prime methods. This certainly is a method that has been adopted by some companies over time and is based on the idea of matching the most current costs against current sales. It is *not* based on the way a company would actually move its inventory physically. The reason that the LIFO method has not gained greater acceptance is the fact that, in the past, there had to be conformity between the way inventories under LIFO were reported for tax purposes as well as the way they were recorded for financial accounting purposes. That is to say, the Internal Revenue Code required that, if a taxpayer was going to use LIFO for tax return purposes, the same method had to be used for financial statement purposes.

What does this mean? Essentially it means that in an environment of rising prices, the taxpayer who wanted to use this method so as to report lower taxable income to the Internal Revenue Service would also have to report lower earnings to shareholders. It is for this reason that LIFO probably has had a lesser degree of acceptance than one would assume. However, all that having been said, many large corporations went to the LIFO method when double-digit inflation occurred in the United States and people wanted the benefit of reporting much lower incomes on their tax returns.

From a managerial accounting standpoint, the inventory issues more often occur at the level of what elements go into the determination of overall cost. By that we mean the cost of an item of inventory includes not only the cost of the materials to manufacture the product but also the cost of the labor that goes into it and the overhead costs that, while not directly related to a particular item of inventory, are elements in determining what it costs to make a product. (By "overhead costs" are meant the costs of manufacturing a product other than the costs of the raw materials and labor going directly into the product. Overhead includes, for example, depreciation costs of the machinery used to make the product.)

For example, depreciation of the factory building in which production takes place is not related to a particular item of inventory produced, yet is often a key part of the total cost structure that has to be taken into account. We will see this in a bit more detail in the portion of this book dealing with basic costing systems.

From a tax standpoint, the determination of cost involving materials, labor, and overhead has a significant impact on the tax liability. Every item of cost that cannot be written off at the time incurred, but must be used in the costing of inventory on hand at the end of the year, increases taxable income. Over time there have been continual battles between taxpayers and the Internal Revenue Service with regard to what types of cost must be capitalized and what can be written off during the current period (called a period cost). In recent years, the Internal Revenue Code has put greater stress on capitalizing more of these costs than was its practice in the past.[4] Taxpayers, therefore, are now getting used to expecting higher tax liabilities because more inventory costs must be deferred to future periods.

The immediate impact this has on the business is the need for construction of an accounting information system that keeps track of capitalization in accordance not only with the Internal Revenue Code and the corresponding regulations but also with those rules that exist for the managerial accounting records used for the operations of the business. Coincidentally, the computer age perhaps is the only age within which multiple uses of cost information of this type could be done. The objective is to record an item of accounting information only once but to accumulate such items and then to extract different types of information out of the overall system for financial accounting, managerial accounting, and income tax purposes.

One final point with regard to inventories involves the determination of quantities. In this connection there are basically two methods in accounting terminology: the Perpetual Inventory method and the Periodic Inventory method. The Perpetual Inventory method assumes that when an item of inventory is sold, a record is adjusted on a realtime basis, so that the company has a continuous record of inventory on hand. In situations where inventory items of large value and few quantities are involved (e.g., 747 airplanes), this method provides a reasonable way for handling the business. On the other hand, in a business that manufactures many items of small value (e.g., toothbrushes), it is very often not practical to use the Perpetual Inventory system. In this case, a Periodic system relies heavily on physically counting the inventory at some point in the accounting cycle, costing out that inventory on whatever method has been adopted, and subtracting that quantity from total inventory at the beginning of the year plus purchases during the year. In effect, this method determines what the inventory costs for the current period are based on a quantity computed in this indirect way.

With the aid of computers, however, more companies have gained the capability of keeping track of large quantities of items and have been able to use (or are considering using) the Perpetual method. From a managerial accounting standpoint, operating people will certainly rely more on a Perpetual method of some type because it is essential for them to be able to ensure they have sufficient inventory on hand to service their customers in a timely and efficient manner. For this reason, it may be cost effective to adopt a system of this type for internal operations where it might not be required for financial accounting to outside parties.

For companies in the retail industry, there are methods set up (called the Retail Inventory method) that essentially keep track of inventory by the retail sales price of the item. The idea, without going into detail, is that an easier way of determining what the items cost is to determine the sales price and then to backing into the cost of the item by utilizing statistics accumulated during the accounting period between the cost of purchases and the selling prices. Such a method, however, normally has to be double-checked by actually having physical inventories at some point in time so that records that are maintained are brought into line with what actually exists in physical inventory.

Other than the new capitalization rules in the Internal Revenue Code, the tax rules generally do not go into specifics as to how costs are to be computed. However, the one system the IRS does not permit is a standard cost system whereby inventory is costed only on the basis of hypothetical costs based on what the inventory should cost assuming certain efficient levels of production. We will see more of this in the managerial accounting area of this book, where standard costs are a normal technique used for relieving inventories when items are sold or otherwise disposed of. Standard accounting systems are excellent techniques for use in calculating variances between the budgeted and actual results of a company in determining how efficient a company is in its production methods. (The term "variance" relates to the difference between the costs a company anticipated in producing a product and what it actually costs. This technique is very often used in the management of a business to compare efficiencies in obtaining the best prices a product or in manufacturing it in the most efficient way.)

CHAPTER PERSPECTIVE

In this chapter we have begun the discussion of the various elements that make up the attributes of a business. We have looked at the resources of the business, for which we use the term "assets." We have seen that assets have a variety of qualities, some of them being of very short duration and others having a long-term value to the company.

We have seen that accounting standards tend to rely very heavily on recording assets at the historical cost and do not seek to value them at fair market value every day of the year. In this way, the accounting system provides a certain consistency in treatment while, at the other hand, having some deficiencies in their utilization.

We have also seen in this chapter that accounting conservatism will tend to understate rather than overstate assets at any particular point in time.

In the area of inventories, there are a number of ways of computing the cost of an inventory. Which of these methods is chosen by a firm depends on the firm's objectives: whether management wants to favor the value on a balance sheet or whether they want to concentrate on inventory costs in the annual income statement.

You have also seen in this chapter the fact that tax rules vary from accounting rules: consequently, overall business planning has to take both of those situations into account.

FOOTNOTES

1 *"Reporting Income, Cash Flows and Financial Position of Business Enterprises" Statement of Financial Accounting Concepts (Stamford, CT: FASB, 1981), para. 29.*

2 *Ibid, para. 25.*

3 *"Get It Off The Balance Sheet" Richard Dieter and Arthur R. Watt, Financial Executive (Volume 48, June 1980)*

4 *UNICAP rules as set forth in Internal Revenue Code Section 263A and the Regulations thereunder.*

Long-Term Assets

INTRODUCTION AND MAIN POINTS

In this chapter we will round out our discussion of the assets that produce the revenues of a business. Having laid the groundwork in the previous chapter in our coverage of short term assets, we can now delve into the subject of long-term assets.

After studying the material in this chapter;

■ You will have a grasp of the major differences between accounting for long-term assets and accounting for short-term assets.

■ You will understand the basis on which long-term assets are recorded on financial statements.

■ You will have an appreciation for the way in which those costs of fixed assets are spread over the years they will be expected to last in the use of the business.

■ You will understand the accounting treatment of the disposition of these long-term assets and the impact it has on the financial results of the business.

■ You will appreciate the significance that intangible assets have on the future of the business and, in particular, the manner in which these intangible assets are reflected in financial statements.

■ You will have an introduction to the Return of Investment (ROI) calculation used in fixed asset evaluation.

Contrasted with the current assets described in Chapter 2, long-term assets are those assets that have a life cycle of longer than one year or the operating cycle of a company, whichever is longer. The basic significance of this factor is that such expenditures are not written off, and thus do not reduce net income of the company, in the period they are acquired. Rather, their cost is spread over future periods—estimated useful life of each asset— in some orderly fashion so that the income generated through the utilization of these assets bears a portion of their cost. The most obvious example of this is equipment that a company acquires to manufacture its products. Such equipment often has a relatively long life, depending on such factors as physical wear and tear and, more importantly in recent years, obsolescence.

From a financial accounting standpoint, GAAP requires that the cost of such assets be accumulated at the time they are purchased or constructed. These costs would include the purchase price of the asset itself, the cost of installing the item in place to function in the business, and indeed all costs that relate to putting the equipment or other asset in a position to function in a commercial way. The accounting issues involved are complicated when the asset is paid for through the issuance of debt obligations. In these instances the costs of the assets are impacted to some extent by the terms of the liabilities that are incurred in order to finance the equipment—deferred payment contracts, discounted bonds payable, and other financing techniques. (By *deferred payment contracts* is meant a financial arrangement in which the payments for an asset are not made immediately at the time of acquisition but, rather, are stretched out into the future. *Discounted bonds payable* indicates a financing arrangement whereby the fair market value of a bond is less than the face value on the bond. This is generally due to the fact that the interest rate the bond carries is less than the going rate of interest.) Companies interested in increasing net income will very often try to capitalize as much of these costs as possible in order to spread them over the future life of the asset.

From a tax standpoint, however, the opposite tendency would be prevalent. That is, the taxpayer would want to write off as a deductible expense as many of the costs related to the asset as possible so as to keep the current tax liability to the irreducible minimum. To illustrate this simply, peruse the following comparison:

Lydia Company acquires a machine for $500,000. Its useful life for accounting purposes is decided to be 20 years, but for tax purposes IRS guidelines would permit a write-off over a shorter period—say, 10 years.

Here is what Lydia Company's abbreviated income and tax statements would look like:

	Financial Statement	Tax Return
Net income before depreciation	$100,000	$100,000
Depreciation of the new machine	25,000	50,000
Net income before taxes	$ 75,000	$ 50,000

From a managerial accounting standpoint, the cost of long-term assets enters into their computation of return on investment (ROI) and other measurement standards. (*Return on investment* means the percentage that is computed by dividing the income from a particular investment by the cost of that investment.) Thus, a dollar of cost that is added to the asset acquired forms the basis of the computation of return on investment but also increases the income that enters into that computation. Consequently, to the extent to which a company wants to measure the return on investment of an asset or, more likely, a group of assets in a production line, it will assist the computation and produce a higher figure if a dollar of expense is removed from the numerator and put in the denominator of the fraction. This is illustrated below:

ROI COMPUTATION

	Situation 1	Situation 2
Net income	100,000	200,000
Divided by:	—	—
Assets:	1,000,000	1,100,000
Equals:		
ROI:	10%	18%

METHODS OF DEPRECIATION

The methods of accounting for long-term assets involved not only the method of depreciation used but also the assumed life of the asset. Depreciation from a financial accounting standpoint is not intended solely to take into account the physical deterioration of the asset as much as to be a systematic method of allocating the historical costs incurred over the asset's useful life. Many methods are available, including the straight-line method, the units-of-production method, accelerated depreciation, and various types of usage experience. (*Accelerated depreciation* means recording as the cost of a fixed asset over its useful life an amount that is in excess of what would be determined by the *straight-line method,* which spreads that cost evenly over each year in the life of the asset. Thus, the straight-line method simply (1) computes the cost of the asset, (2) subtracts the estimated salvage value at the end of its life, and (3) divides the result by the number of years its life is estimated to last.)

The units-of-production method tries to relate the write-off of an asset to its overall expected output, as opposed to the period of time it is estimated to last. Accelerated methods, such as declining balance depreciation, attempt to give recognition to the fact that more of an asset's cost utilization takes place in its early years than in its later years. The accelerated methods, in truth, are more attractive for tax purposes than for accounting purposes. To the extent that the tax law permits the taxpayer to write off assets more quickly, the tax deductions are higher and the taxable income is lower. In a company that is expanding and adding new assets on a regular basis, the accelerated methods enable a taxpayer to manage its tax liability in a more cost-effective way. Unlike the methods of handling LIFO inventories (discussed in Chapter 2), there is no requirement in the Internal Revenue Code that the taxpayer conform the financial accounting for depreciation with the tax accounting. Consequently, significant differences are experienced, as discussed in Chapter 6. For our purposes here, a useful example of this type of accounting is found in a footnote from the annual report of General Electric Company, reproduced below:

General Electric Company
Statement of Financial Position (in millions)

	1983	1982
Property, plant, and equipment - net (note 11)	$ 7,697	$ 7,308
Summary of Significant Accounting Policies		
Depreciation, depletion, and amortization.		

The cost of most manufacturing plant and equipment is depreciated using an accelerated method based primarily on a sum-of-the years' digits formula. If manufacturing plant and equipment is subject to abnormal economic conditions or obsolescence, additional depreciation is provided. The cost of mining properties is depreciated, depleted or amortized mainly by the unit-of-production method. Mining exploration costs are charged directly to expense until development of a specific mineral deposit is likely to be economically feasible. After this determination, all related development costs are capitalized and subsequently amortized over the productive life of the property, commencing with the start-up of production. The full-cost accounting method is used for oil and gas properties.

Notes to Financial Statements

11 Property, plant, and equipment

(in millions)	1983	1982
Major classes at December 31:		
Manufacturing plant and equipment		
Land and improvements	$ 192	$ 188
Buildings, structures, and related equipment	2,965	2,851
Machinery and equipment	8,533	7,884
Leasehold costs and manufacturing plant under construction	578	424
Mineral property, plant, and equipment	2,538	2,496
	$14,806	$13,843
Cost at January 1	$13,843	$12,705
Additions	1,721	1,608
Dispositions	(758)	(470)
Cost at December 31	$14,806	$13,843
Accumulated depreciation, depletion, and amortization		
Balance at January 1	$ 6,535	$ 5,861
Current-year provision	1,084	984
Dispositions	(507)	(304)
Other changes	(3)	(6)
Balance at December 31	$ 7,109	$ 6,535

The statement of the financial position of the General Electric Company, reprinted below, illustrates the different types of methods that can be utilized by companies for depreciation purposes. It provides the reader with a good overview of alternatives available in the real world.

Annual Charges for Depreciation
Under Declining Balance and Sum of Digits Methods
Compared with Straight-Line Method
(Assumed Depreciation Base, $100,000)

10-year life	Straight line	Declining balance(A)	Sum of digits (B)	Excess over straight line Declining balance	Excess over straight line Sum of digits
	$ 10,000	$ 20,000	$ 18,182	$10,000	$ 8,182
	10,000	16,000	16,364	6,000	6,364
	10,000	12,800	14,545	2,800	4,545
	10,000	10,240	12,747	240	2,727
	10,000	8,192	10,909	(1,808)	909
	10,000	6,554	9,091	(3,446)	(909)
	10,000	6,554	7,273	(3,446)	(2,727)
	10,000	6,554	5,455	(3,446)	(4,545)
	10,000	6,553	3,636	(3,447)	(6,364)
10	10,000	6,553	1,818	(3,447)	(6,182)
Totals	$100,000	$100,000	$100,000	-0-	-0-

(A) Computed by determining the percent under the straight line method ($100,000 ÷ 10 yrs = $10,000 per year ÷ 100,000 asset cost = 10%) and then multiplying this percentage by some multiple (e.g. 10% x 200% = 20%). This new percent is then used each year times the declining balance.

(B) Computed by adding of the digits representing each year of the assets life (e.g. 1 + 2 + 3 . . . + 10 = 55) and using that as the denominator of a fraction with the numerator being the digits for the years in declining order (e.g.

$$\frac{10 \times 100,000}{55} = 18,182 \text{ for year \#1)}$$

From a managerial accounting standpoint, great attention tends to be paid to assigning the cost of a long-term asset to the production or sales results than to the utilization of that asset. Therefore, there can be major differences between managerial and financial accounting in this area. There would be no problem, for example, for a company to decide to write off the entire cost of an asset in the period incurred, if it were doing so for managerial accounting reasons that were logical—for example, in the case of an asset that will be utilized for only one project and will be consumed entirely for this project. It is unlikely that this would be done, but it is possible. This, however, would probably not be acceptable either for financial accounting purposes or for tax accounting purposes.

USEFUL LIFE

Different assets have different useful lives. For example, at one end of the asset-life continuum is land, which is considered to have an indefinite life and is therefore not depreciated.

The matter of estimating useful life and thus determining the period of time for depreciation is complicated. One's initial inclination is generally to assume that useful life spans just the time in which the wear and tear of using the machine will render it useless. However, in today's high-tech environment, obsolescence is becoming more and more the issue of how long an asset will last. Many assets that are still physically able to operate have been rendered obsolete by new technology. (Have you bought your *second* personal computer yet?) This means that the company should take into account the obsolescence factor in addition to the physical wear and tear in coming up with a useful life for depreciation.

This is a highly contested area in income tax preparation, where obsolescence is an appropriate factor to consider but where there are sharp differences of opinion between taxpayers and the Internal Revenue Service as to how severe obsolescence will become. Historical experience is generally relied upon as an indicator of how reliable and reasonable the taxpayers' arguments would be viewed.

The tax accounting rules have their own requirements for what the useful life of an asset might be. These rules have changed over time as the government has decided either to encourage people to purchase capital assets by offering more generous tax deductions or to retard such purchases by eliminating the higher deductions.

The tax rules here are extremely detailed, but it should be sufficient for the reader to understand that the useful lives specified in publications from the Treasury Department will not be challenged by the Internal Revenue Service. To the extent that taxpayers have situations in which they believe the assets will be utilized in a shorter period of time, they have the opportunity of taking tax deductions at a quicker rate than those prescribed in the guidelines produced by the government. However, it is likely that these will be challenged by the Internal Revenue Service so that such taxpayers will have to prove the reason for taking a deduction at a faster rate than that allowed by the government publications. (More detailed information on the government issue guidelines can be found under Section 167 of the Internal Revenue Code.)

DISPOSITIONS

The disposition of long-term assets is another factor that has to be considered. Very often such assets will be disposed of at a price that varies from the price at which they were carried on the books (particularly after years of depreciation accumulation). Where disposition takes place for cash, there is generally less confusion than when assets are traded in for other assets. The following is a comparative example of this situation.

Long-term Asset Disposition

For Cash:

Receive cash		$1,000
Original cost	$5,000	
Less depreciation	4,500	
Adjusted cost		500
Gain		500

Trade in:

Original cost	5,000	
Less depreciation	4,500	
Adjusted cost		500
Book value of new asset		500

From a financial accounting standpoint, such gains or losses may or may not be recognized. Thus, one rule is that where exchanges of similar nonmonetary assets occur, the earning process is not considered completed, thus a gain should not be recognized. However, if the exchange transactions involve similar assets and would result in a loss, the loss is recognized immediately. Again, this is a factor attributable to the conservatism of the accounting rules.

From a tax standpoint, there is also the general rule that the disposition of an asset requires the recognition of a gain or a loss, but where like kind exchanges take place, there is also the ability to defer the gain or the loss to some point in the future.[1]

INTANGIBLES

With regard to intangible assets of long life, there is significant disagreement between those that are purchased and those that are created by the business itself. (The term *intangible assets* refers to fixed assets that are of different character than physical assets—a company's buildings, machinery, land, equipment, and other assets of a tangible nature.) The rules with regard to cost determination, useful life, and depreciation also apply to intangible assets, since they are significant business assets. For example, the basic rule is that, as in the case of physical assets, the purchase price of a patent, which has a legal life, should be spread over the patent's future life. However, where a patent is developed by a company through its internal research, those costs are generally treated as expenses of the period incurred and are not capitalized. These rules will often be disregarded from a managerial standpoint where other departments of the company are charged for the value of an intangible asset developed by the R&D department. This enables R&D to compute a "profit" on its research activity (or at least a reduction of its loss) while at the same time attributing to the operating divisions using the intangible assets the effect of the fact that such assets are a legitimate cost element for their operation.

From a tax standpoint, there are rules with regard to amortization of intangible assets that do not allow a taxpayer to write off as a tax deduction all the intangible asset costs in the year they are incurred. In connection with intangible assets created by the taxpayer, there are specific tax rules dealing with the write-off of research and development costs which, if they had not been enacted, would require some type of capitalization and spreading the cost over future years.[2]

There are certain intangible assets that may not be written off or have any tax effect until the life of the company is terminated. Goodwill is a good example of this type of cost. (*Goodwill* is a complicated fixed asset. The idea is that certain companies are able to earn a rate of profit that exceeds what might be considered a normal profit for a business of its size. These excess profits, then, give the business a greater return on investment than normal. Goodwill is the present value of the future flow of these excess profits.) Similar to the land costs described above, goodwill is considered to have an indefinite useful life. Consequently, no tax deduction is attributable to spreading the costs of these assets over a period prior to disposition. The financial accounting rules are applied to land in one way and in a different way to goodwill in certain instances. For example, where a company acquires another company at a price that exceeds the book value (assets minus liabilities) of the acquired company, accounting conventions generally require that a goodwill amount be computed and spread over some useful period not to exceed 40 years.[3] This produces an expense for financial statement purposes that does not have a comparable tax deduction attributable to it. The following illustrates how such goodwill arises from an acquisition of a company:

Purchase Price by Company A for Company B $1,000,000

Balance Sheet of Company B

Assets	1,000,000	Liabilities	200,000
		Equity	800,000
	1,000,000		1,000,000
Purchase price for B			1,000,000
Less book value for B			800,000
Goodwill			200,000

From a managerial accounting standpoint, intangible assets of this type are very often not assigned to operating departments and divisions. Consequently, they may not enter into the measurement of performance. If this is the case, then they cease to be an important factor in the accounting system utilized for operational purposes. Such assets can, however, have an impact on the measurement of the performance of the R&D group.

COMPUTER COSTS

One particular area that has received a lot of attention is accounting for computer software costs. Since such costs are becoming quite large, businesspeople often like to spread the cost over future years so they can show higher profits for the year in which such costs are actually incurred. Taxation, again, was the instigator of significant discussion on this subject and has resulted in a rule that does allow computer software costs developed internally to be written off on an as-incurred basis.[5] In an attempt to resolve this issue from a financial accounting standpoint, the FASB issued a statement that takes a conservative position that requires the developer to expense all costs of computer software until it has been completed. All planning, designing, coding, and testing activities that are necessary to establish that the product can be produced to meet its designed specifications are expensed. This, however, applies only where the software is to be sold. If the computer software is purchased and it has alternative future uses, then it may be capitalized thereby increasing profits. In addition, this standard does not apply to situations where the business has developed the computer software for its own use and not for sale to third parties.

LEASEHOLD COSTS

In addition to constructing or purchasing a building, many firms will rent real estate premises. In addition, a firm may put certain improvements into the rented property that the company itself owns. These items are called leasehold improvements. In such cases, even though the business does not own the building itself, it does own the leasehold improvements and is entitled to depreciate those improvements for tax as well as accounting purposes. The question is, what type of life is used for depreciating such leasehold improvements?

If we take the situation where an improvement having a life of ten years is attached to premises where the lease term is only five years, the accounting standard would require that the asset be depreciated over the shorter period. This is because it is not certain whether and to what extent the lease can be extended.

On the other hand, if the lease terms give the lessee the option to extend the lease, then these extension periods would be taken into account. Consequently, in the above example, if the lessee has an option to extend the lease for at least five more years (thus resulting in an overall lease term of a minimum of ten years), then it would be appropriate to depreciate the leasehold improvements over the ten-year period. The tax rules dealing with the subject of leasehold improvements have a similar effect in determining when tax depreciation may be taken.

CHAPTER PERSPECTIVE

In this chapter we have expanded the discussion of assets used by a business and have rounded out the discussion on the total resources side of the balance sheet. That is, we have been able to get our arms around how the major assets in a company are treated from an accounting and from a taxation standpoint.

We have seen how costs of long-term assets are determined, how they are depreciated over the life of the asset, how dispositions are treated, and how the growing importance of intangible assets are handled.

Now that we have some feeling for how the assets that produce the income for a company are to be treated, we are in a position to look at the accounting and tax treatment of the liabilities that a business incurs in order to finance such assets.

FOOTNOTES

1 *Internal Revenue Code (IRC) Section 1031*

2 *Internal Revenue Code (IRC) Section 162*

3 *"Intangible Assets," Opinions of the Accounting Principles Board No. 17 (New York: AICPA, 1970), par.27.*

4 *"Accounting for the Costs of Computer Software To Be Sold, Leased, or Otherwise Marketed," Statement of Financial Accounting Standards No. 86 (Stamford, CT: FASB, 1985).*

The Debt Structure of a Business

INTRODUCTION AND MAIN POINTS

In this chapter we will begin studying the way in which debt is incurred by a business and how it is accounted for in determining the firm's net income from an accounting and tax standpoint. Because of the financial obligations that debt imposes on a company, it will be important to see the way in which it is measured in determining whether or not the company is profitable.

After studying the material in this chapter:

 You will have an appreciation of what constitutes liabilities in the first instance.

 You will understand the different types of liabilities that a company can incur and the classification of debt into short-term and long-term liabilities.

 You will have a feeling for the important area of contingencies in a company's activity, enabling you to determine when and to what extent potential liabilities must be reflected in the financial statements.

 You will have achieved an understanding of how the conversion of debt is to be recorded, particularly in those situations where a company is in difficulty and has to restructure its financing.

 You will have developed an understanding of how debt is to be recorded at the time it is issued as well as how it is treated for financial-statement and tax purposes when it is retired.

 You will be able to appreciate the extent to which off-balance-sheet financing has been engaged in by companies and how such items are to be interpreted by you in your evaluation of a company that you are interested in acquiring.

Liabilities are an extremely important and complex factor on the balance sheet of a company, as illustrated by the following excerpt from a report by the Midlantic Corporation:

	1987	1986
Liabilities and shareholders' equity		
Domestic deposits:		
Noninterest-bearing demand	$ 3,629,435	$ 4,146,748
Interest-bearing demand	1,047,528	956,313
Savings	1,837,850	1,720,633
Retail money market account	2,464,129	2,606,456
Money market CD's over $100,000	1,591,866	1,260,078
Other time	2,934,313	2,738,956
Overseas branch deposits	133,117	113,023
Total deposits	$13,638,238	$13,542,207
Bank acceptances outstanding	$ 229,596	$ 221,536
Short term borrowing	2,249,337	1,953,415
Accrued taxes and other liabilities	256,221	256,234
Long-term debt	259,683	214,837
Total liabilities	$16,633,075	$16,188,229

The question "What is a liability?" is not as easy to answer as one would think. If is of course clear that liabilities include debts arising from borrowings. The acquisition of goods or services on credit terms also gives rise to liabilities. Less familiar are liabilities resulting from the imposition of taxes, withholding taxes and other sums from employees' wages and salaries, dividend declarations, and product warranties. In some instances, one might even ask whether preferred stock is in reality a liability or an ownership claim. For decades the official definition of liabilities has been stated in terms of the rules and procedures of accounting—and they have been deficient.

As a result, the liability section of the balance sheet has degenerated into a catchall for all leftover credit balances, some of them ill-conceived.[1]

As in the case with assets discussed in chapters 2 and 3, liabilities have been divided between current and long-term. Current liabilities essentially are those that must be paid within one year or the operating cycle of the company if longer. These would include such items as:

accounts payable to suppliers	notes payable to lenders
short-term obligations	current liabilities not expected to be refinanced
dividends payable	returnable deposits
liability on the advance sale of tickets	tokens and certificates
collections for third parties	accrued liabilities and conditional payments.

contingencies.

(By accrued liabilities is meant the expenses that have arisen but have not yet been recorded. An example would be compensation of employees that have worked but have not yet been paid at the time the financial statement is to be created.)

The "contingencies" item is particularly troublesome because in addition to raising questions about the quantity of the liability, it raises the issue of when the liability should be reflected in the financial statements from an accounting standpoint. An estimated loss from a contingency should be accrued by reflecting an expense and a liability *only* if both of the following conditions are met.

1. Information available prior to the issuance of the financial statements indicates it is *probable* that a liability has been incurred at the date of the financial statements.

2. The amount of the loss can be *reasonably estimated.*[2]

If a picture is worth a thousand words, then Figure 4-1 gives the reader some idea of the panoply of losses and whether they are usually accrued in the financial statements, not accrued or fall into a kind of no-man's land of possibly being accrued.

	Usually Accrued	Not Accrued	Maybe Accrued
Loss Related to:			
1. Collectibility of receivables	X		
2. Obligations related to product warranties and product defects	X		
3. Premiums offered to customers	X		
4. Risk of loss or damage of enterprise property by fire, explosion, or other hazards		X	
5. General or unspecified business risk		X	
6. Risk of loss from catastrophes assumed by property and casualty insurance companies including reinsurance companies	X		
7. Threat of expropriation of assets			X
8. Pending or threatened litigation			X
9. Actual or possible claims and assessments			X
10. Guarantees of indebtedness of others			X
11. Obligations of commercial banks under "Standby letters of credit"			X
12. Agreements to repurchase receivables (or the related property) that have been sold			X

FIG. 4-1 *Accounting Treatment of Loss Contingencies*

Where an item such as a contingency is not to be accrued on the books, it very often is disclosed in footnotes to the financial statements for accounting purposes. Set forth below is an example of this as it relates to CBS, Inc.

LITIGATION
The Company is named as a defendant in numerous defamation actions in the United States, including an action (discussed below) commenced by William C. Westmoreland on September 13, 1982, in the United States District Court for the District of South Carolina. While the Company cannot predict the results of these actions, it believes that it has meritorious defenses and that the liability, if any, resulting from

such suits will be substantially covered by insurance and that any uninsured liability from such actions will not have a materially adverse effect on its consolidated operations or consolidated financial position.

In the action referred to above, William C. Westmoreland claims a total of $120 million in compensatory and punitive damages as a result of alleged defamations by a CBS news Special Report entitled "The Uncounted Enemy; a Vietnam Deception," broadcast by CBS on January 23, 1982 and by related broadcasts and publications. CBS has denied the material allegations of the complaint and successfully brought transfer of the action to the United States District Court for the Southern District of New York, where the matter is now pending and in discovery.

From a tax standpoint, the recording of short-term liabilities very often gives rise to expenses that are deductible from taxable income. The Internal Revenue Code requirements are stricter than the financial accounting rules described above because they try to deter taxpayers from taking deductions for things that are only probably payable at the present time.[3] Purchases of goods and services are very often not areas of major controversy. But where a taxpayer has *potentially* incurred a liability but all events have not been settled with regard to either its existence or its amount, there will be difficulties with the Internal Revenue Service.

From a managerial accounting standpoint, such liabilities often impact the measurement of performance where the question of a liability occurrence is up in the air. No operating executive wants to have his or her results put into question by recording all possible liabilities that could occur. However, pushing these items off into the indefinite future does not give a clear picture of the performance of the department or division. Managerial accounting rules, therefore, can vary from financial accounting rules because FASB requirements do not necessarily apply in managerial accounting.

LONG-TERM LIABILITIES

The area of long-term debt is even more complicated because of the innovative financing packages that have been created over the recent decade. In the past, debt financing has been supplemented by financing with "equity kickers," interest rate swaps, currency swaps, and a variety of items that are part debt but also part equity. (By an *equity kicker* is meant financing involving primarily debt but in which the investor, in addition, gets some kind of interest or potential interest in the ownership of the business. Thus, in addition to the debt instrument he may acquire, he also gets an equity instrument. An *interest rate swap* is a financing arrangement in which an investor exchanges or swaps his obligation at one rate of interest for one at another rate of interest. *Currency swaps* are somewhat similar to interest rate swaps in that a person would exchange or swap a debt in one currency for an obligation in some other currency. This is a common type of transaction for businesses involved in foreign countries.)

Because of the dynamism of this subject it has caused a crossing over of activities among commercial banks, investment banks, the securities industry, the insurance industry, and several other financial-service organizations. This competition, coupled with the sophisticated communication systems that exist today, has provided areas where there is no "seam" between one deal and another. As a result, it raises such fundamental questions as What is the need for a service organization to serve as intermediary between the borrower of funds and the lender of the funds? Why can't the two parties do business with each other directly? The advent of commercial paper in the recent past is a good reason for this type of question. The fact that the Glass-Stegall law—the legislation that requires businesses engaged in banking or similar financial industries to be restricted to that type of activity—is open for repeal further confuses this subject. For example, at the present time in the United States, a banking institution cannot engage in brokerage activity and vice versa.

Entire books have been written on the subject of financing, so our role here will be to present an overview of some major accounting and tax aspects involving the issuance of debt, the retirement of debt, and the conversion of debt into other securities.

ISSUANCE OF DEBT

From the standpoint of financial accounting, the issuance of debt has as its first complication the question of what the value of the debt issued actually is. For example, in prior, less sophisticated accounting environments, if a $1,000 bond was issued for $900 and was to be outstanding for ten years, the $100 difference (called discount) was divided by 10 and subtracted from earnings equally each year. There is now a more sophisticated and effective interest method of amortizing such a discount, as specified in GAAP. It has as its objective subtracting the discount from earnings in a manner that reflects a constant interest rate on the amount of the balance of the debt outstanding. The following table illustrates how the interest expense is computed using the effective interest rate method. You will see from this demonstration that, instead of the discount on the borrowing being spread evenly over each year in which the debt is outstanding, the amount varies. However, what does remain constant is the rate of interest being imposed on the debt as the principal amount of the debt declines over the course of the years.

Maturity value of bonds payable	$100,000
Present value of $100,000 due in 5 years at 10%, interest payable semiannually; a (p $\overline{10}$ 5%); ($100,000 × .61391)	$61,391
Present value of $4,000 interest payable semiannually for 5 years at 10% annually; R (P $\overline{10}$ 5%); ($4,000 × 7.72173)	30,887
Proceeds from sale of bonds	92,278
Discount on bonds payable	$ 7,722

The five-year amortization schedule appears in Table 4-1.

TABLE 4-1
SCHEDULE OF BOND DISCOUNT AMORTIZATION
EFFECTIVE INTEREST METHOD - SEMIANNUAL INTEREST
PAYMENTS
5-YEAR, 8% BONDS SOLD TO YIELD 10%

Date	Credit Cash	Debit Interest Expense	Credit Bond Discount	Carrying Amount of Bonds
1/1/86				$ 92,278
7/1/86	$ 4,000[a]	$ 4,614[b]	$ 614[c]	92,892[d]
1/1/87	4,000	4,645	645	93,537
7/1/87	4,000	4,677	677	94,214
1/1/88	4,000	4,711	711	94,925
7/1/88	4,000	4,746	746	95,671
1/1/89	4,000	4,783	783	96,454
7/1/89	4,000	4,823	823	97,277
1/1/90	4,000	4,864	864	98,141
7/1/90	4,000	4,907	907	99,048
1/1/91	4,000	4,952	952	100,000
	$40,000	$47,722	$7,722	

[a]$4,000 = $100,000 × .08 × 6/12   [c]$614 = $4,614 − $4,000
[b]$4,614 = $ 92,278 × .10 × 6/12   [d]$92,892 = $92,278 + $614

From a tax standpoint, issuing debt at a discount requires the taxpayer to reflect the fact that the original issue discount (OID) is really an interest factor. For that reason an investor in such debt instruments cannot treat the entire amount received upon payment of the debt as a capital gain. This was a loophole long since plugged by the Congress. The essence of the idea, however, is important. That is, regardless of the par (face) value of bonds, the going rate of interest in the market determines the fair market value of those bonds. This in turn determines whether there is a premium or a discount on the issuance. (By a *premium* on a bond is meant that the bond is issued for an amount in excess of the par value; by *discount* is meant that, at the time of issuance, a bond carries a price that is less than its par value.) The premium and discount factors enter into the calculations of what the real interest rate is on the bonds. This determines the deductibility for the bond issuer and the income to be reported by the investor.

From a managerial accounting standpoint, the issuance of long-term debt becomes relevant in a derivative way. This is to say that the operating divisions will generally be charged an interest factor for the utilization of resources. This factor, in turn, is determined by the going rate for funds for the organization as a whole. Arguments will arise as to whether the subdivision of the company could do a better job of raising capital, but generally this is a nonnegotiable issue for the head office people.

This also brings up the question of performance measurement. If the operating people do not have control over the fund-raising factor (other than not acquiring assets that would be paid for with the borrowed funds), can they be effectively charged for the responsibility of that element in their income statement? At this point the discussion becomes less a matter of accounting and more a fundamental question of management system organization, a subject we will cover in a later chapter on cost and profit center evaluations.

RETIREMENT OF DEBT

From the standpoint of debt retirement, gains or losses arise measured by the difference between the carrying value of the debt and the fair market value of the consideration used to extinguish it. (The *carrying value* of a debt means the amount at which it is reflected in the financial statements. This would normally be the original issuance price adjusted by the amortization of premium or discount on the bond over its outstanding life to the present time.) Because of the troubled financial situations that many companies eventually face, the restructuring of debt has become a sophisticated art. One important area is that of the "insubstance defeasance." This constitutes the setting aside of a certain body of assets that can be utilized to service a debt outstanding on the books of the company. The objective is to get the debt off the company's books, and it makes particularly good sense when the interest rates on the assets set aside can be used to service an amount of debt that is larger than the value of the assets. A significant degree of controversy exists as to whether and to what extent this method should be permitted for accounting purposes; it remains an area on which there is significant disagreement. At the end of the day, however, it is a manifestation of the sophistication to which the treatment of troubled debt has arisen. An example will help as to how the determination of a loss or gain on retirement of debt might be computed. The following table will illustrate the point; it relates the reacquisition price of the debt to the net carrying amount of the bonds redeemed.

Reacquisition price ($800,000 × 101)		$808,000
Net carrying amount of bonds redeemed:		
Face value	$800,000	
Unamortized discount ($24,000 × 10/20)	(12,000)	
Unamortized issue costs ($16,000 × 10/20)		
(both amortized using straight-line basis)	(8,000)	780,000
Loss on redemption		$ 28,000

The entry to record the reacquisition and cancellation of the bonds is:

Bonds payable	800,000	
Loss on redemption of bonds (extraordinary)	28,000	
Discount on bonds payable		12,000
Unamortized bond issue costs		8,000
Cash		808,000

From a tax standpoint, retirement of debt also gives rise to gains and losses that will impact the taxable income of the entity. As mentioned earlier, original-issue discount is a factor that affects the interest income and expense items. As a result, OID will adjust the amount of gain or loss that might be recognized on the retirement. Unless the company is in the business of extinguishing debt (a very rare instance), management will realize a capital gain or loss upon the extinguishment of outstanding debt where the carrying value from a tax standpoint is different from the fair market value of the consideration used to extinguish the debt.

Managerial accounting once again gets impacted tangentially by reason of the effect such extinguishments would have on the overall cost of money to the company, which in turn gets impacted by the financial function of the company's operating divisions. In an indirect way, the issuance and the extinguishment of debt from a managerial accounting standpoint are important factors in determining what value an asset will have when placed on the books. For example, suppose debt is issued at an interest rate of 10% (that being the going rate) and $5 million of bonds are sold at par value for the acquisition of an unproven amount of intangible assets that have been generated by another company's R&D effort. There is no clear way to establish the value for the asset other than what the value would be for the debt issued to acquire it. As a result, operating divisions may find that one technique would be to capitalize the assets they acquire by using the fair market value of the debt incurred as opposed to writing off the assets immediately for divisional or departmental measurement purposes.

CONVERSION OF DEBT

The conversion of debt into other financial instruments produces complications, but these can be dealt with fairly readily in today's environment owing to the frequency with which this often happens. The importance of accounting in these instances lies in obtaining the numbers that are required to reflect the reality of what has happened.

From the financial accounting standpoint, for example, refunding of debt by exchanging one type of debt for another may at times be viewed as merely a substitution of one debt for the other, thus not give rise to any gain or loss in the financial statement. The more conventional approach, however, is to consider this to be a transaction where the difference in the cost of money at the time of the original borrowing and at the time of the conversion would trigger a transaction that will impact the net income of the company.

From the taxation standpoint, conversion of debt very often gives rise to taxable transactions. This can in turn create situations where there is a difference between the financial accounting and tax recording of a transaction. For that reason, close coordination between the finance and tax function in a company is important so that no undue tax "surprises" crop up in connection with a refinancing transaction.

Again, because of a debt conversion's impact on the going cost of money within the organization at a corporate level, this can have derivative effects on operating divisions that need those resources to conduct their activities. Because of the lack of control by production and marketing people over such activities, its utilization by and measurement of the operating units are something that needs careful consideration if it is to be meaningful to the people being measured as well as those doing the measuring.

In connection with the subject of restructuring troubled debt, there is a difference from an accounting standpoint as to whether the item is a settlement of a debt (and therefore treated as a closed transaction) or is a continuation of the debt with a modification in terms. What is the difference? The difference is that, in the former situation, gain and loss are considered properly recorded because a transfer of economic resources occurs as a result of restructuring.

However, where there is a continuation of the existing debt with modification of terms, the carrying amount of the debt is generally not changed, nor will the creditor change the recorded investment in the receivable. One might smile at this treatment, particularly given the notoriety the big U.S. banks' restructuring of debt with Latin American countries has had in the financial press. For all intents and purposes, people will feel that the changing of terms is in reality a transaction that should be reflected in the accounts. The point being noted here, therefore, is that there is flexibility in this area of troubled debt restructuring and it is meaningful to note that financial accounting has a range of possible alternatives. Table 4-2 on the next page presents an overview of this issue of accounting procedures for debt restructuring.

OFF-BALANCE-SHEET FINANCING

One final important area in the discussion of long-term debt deals not with the debt that appears on the books, but rather the off-balance-sheet debt. It has been said in financial circles that the basic drives of humans are few: to get enough food, to find shelter, and to keep debt off the balance sheet! A facetious comment, yes, but nevertheless reflective of the thinking of many executives with regard to how to present the best picture to the outside world, consistent with what a firm's competitors are doing.

TABLE 4-2
SUMMARY OF ACCOUNTING PROCEDURES
FOR TROUBLED DEBT RESTRUCTURINGS

Form of Restructure	Accounting Procedure
Settlement of Debt	
1. Transfer of noncash assets.	1. Recognize gain (debtor) or loss (creditor) on restructure. Debtor recognizes gain or loss on asset transfer.
2. Granting of equity interest.	2. Recognize gain (debtor) or loss (creditor) on restructure.
Continuation of Debt with Modified Terms	
1. Carrying amount of debt is less than total future cash flows.	1. Recognize no gain (loss) on restructure. Determine new effective interest rate to be used in recording interest expense (debtor) and interest revenue (creditor).
2. Carrying amount of debt is greater than total future cash flows.	2. Recognize gain (loss) on restructure.* Recognize no interest expense or revenue over remaining life of debt.

*Recognition of gain or loss here implies that the carrying amount prior to the restructuring will be reduced to an amount equal to the total future cash flows.

Off-balance-sheet financing is a subject all to itself. Our purpose here is to alert the reader to the existence of a range of activities of this type. Four examples are given below:

1. The sale of accounts receivable with recourse, which enables the company, in effect, to borrow money through the medium of selling its receivables.
2. Research and development arrangements whereby an agreement is entered into with another party to engage in certain R&D efforts for which the company will pay, though it will not record on its books the assets or liabilities associated with the research.

3. Project financing arrangements where one company enters into an agreement with another company to run a joint facility, with the assets and liabilities being off the balance sheets of the two partners in the arrangement.
4. Captive finance companies, where a group of people (particularly those in the same industry) agree to form a separate company to finance their needs, again with assets and liabilities of the financing activity being off the books of the participating companies.

These are but a few illustrations of the innovations that have come up in the area.

Why would people do things like this? One reason is that many companies reach the limit imposed by debt covenants on the amount of debt they may have outstanding at any point in time. (A *debt covenant* is the agreement that the company signs when it enters into a debt agreement. It is the contract that exists between the borrower and the lender.) As a result, off-balance-sheet financing is used because it gets around these commitments restricting a company's ability to acquire assets by taking on additional debt. Second, the removal of debt from the balance sheet is considered by some to enhance the quality of a company's balance sheet, allowing credit to be obtained more readily and at a lower cost.

The primary response of FASB to these off-balance-sheet financing arrangements for financial accounting purposes has been to ask for increased disclosure. Whether this is an adequate answer, it at least gives the reader of financial statements some clues as to areas to delve into if he or she wants to make an evaluation of the status of the company in comparison with its competitors or even with its status at different times.

From a tax accounting standpoint, off-balance-sheet financing presents difficulties in discovering transactions that will have significance for tax purposes. "Off balance sheet" may not mean "off tax return." The fact is that the tax system looks to completed transactions for tax-significant events, and many of the off-balance-sheet techniques may well be completed transactions even though they are not reflected on the books of the company. As a result, such transactions can, at times, escape the information system designed to capture all transactions having tax importance. For this reason, it is necessary to have a sophisticated accounting system in order to make certain that, while these transactions may be out of sight, they are not out of mind of people charged with the responsibility of preparing a true and accurate tax return. The emergence of significant penalties in the tax law should be enough reason for people in the company to make certain that appropriate information on these types of transactions is captured and reflected properly for tax purposes.

From a managerial accounting standpoint, having the item off the balance sheet at the corporate level does not necessarily mean that it is out of the consideration of the operating people at the departmental level. For instance, a division that has factored (sold) its receivables has clear in its mind the fact that it has obtained resources for utilization in its operation by a means that could come back to haunt them if it is done on a recourse basis. (*Factoring* is a transaction whereby a company sells an asset such as accounts receivable to a financing party so that the company receives cash before the receivables are collected; that, when a financing transaction is entered into on a *recourse basis*, this means that if the transaction does not materialize the way the parties thought, the lender of the funds can go back and get payment from the borrower.)

Similarly, a joint-venture company may be formed to create a manufacturing facility that is kept off balance sheet from a corporate standpoint, but the joint venture is clearly within the control (and responsibility) of the operating people, who need the new facility's production to help their division to operate efficiently. Consequently, for all intents and purposes managerial accounting must look through these types of transactions to make certain that they have the appropriate numbers to manage their business effectively.

CHAPTER PERSPECTIVE

In this chapter we have delved into the very sophisticated subject of debt financing. It is the part of the business operation in which the owners go to outside parties for additional funds so that they can expand their business. While some business owners would prefer to finance on their own, out of the firm's revenues, they generally realize that if the business is to expand more rapidly, funds are required from outside parties.

We have seen in this chapter what the basic accounting and taxation rules are with regard to the borrowing of funds and the paying of interest on outstanding obligations. We have also seen how the rules operate with regard to the repayment of debt once it has become due. Also, realizing that many businesses have changing circumstances, we have reviewed the rules that apply to restructuring of debt, that is, when debt is exchanged for other debt and also when debt is exchanged for various kinds of other consideration.

Up to this point, we have focused on the way in which assets are acquired through borrowings. We will now take a look in the next chapter at the way the owners of a business have their shares of profits (and losses) reflected in the accounting and taxation reports.

FOOTNOTES

1 *D. E. Kieso and J. J. Weygardt, Intermediate Accounting, 5th ed. (New York: John Wiley & Sons, 1986), p. 535. Et Seq.*

2 *"Accounting for Contingencies" Statement of Financial Accounting Standards No. 5 (Stamford, CT: FASB, 1975), para. 1.*

3 *Treasury Regulations—Section 1.461-1(2).*

Who Owns the Company?

INTRODUCTION AND MAIN POINTS

In this chapter we will complete our study of the major elements of a balance sheet, which is the accounting statement that outlines the condition of a company at a certain point in time. In earlier chapters we have looked at the resources of a company (the assets) as well as the debt obligations that the company has to outside financing sources (liabilities). The remaining part of this equation consists of the portion of the company that is identified by the owners.

After studying the material in this chapter:

━ You will have an appreciation for the ownership of a company, whether it be a small, privately owned company or a large multinational corporation.

━ You will be able to explain the issues involved with a company getting started by issuing shares of stock to outside investors.

━ You will have an understanding of the role that earnings per share play in the evaluation of a company's activities.

━ You will have a rudimentary understanding of the accounting and taxation rules involved in restructuring companies, a phenomenon that has become very prevalent in recent decades in the United States.

━ You will have an understanding of the manner in which the ownership of a company is enhanced, not only by the infusion of resources from the outside but also by the retention of earnings of a company over the years in which it has generated profits.

Although there are fewer corporations than sole proprietorships and partnerships in the United States, the corporate form of business dominates the economy in total dollars of assets and output of goods and services. (The term "proprietorship" means a business that is conducted by one individual; the term "partnership" refers to an association of two or more persons to carry on as co-owners a business for profit.) The major reasons for this dominance is that it is easier for a corporation to amass a large amount of capital as well as the fact that the corporate form of business is well suited for today's trends toward large organizations, international trade, and professional management.

Given our earlier discussions in Chapter 3 and 4 of a company having resources called assets and obligations to outsiders called liabilities, the residue is what belongs to the owners of the business. In the corporate environment this would be the shareholders; in the case of partnerships it would be the several partners who have decided to pool their talents for a venture; and in the case of a sole proprietorship it would be the one person that owns the business.

From the financial accounting standpoint the issuance of capital stock in a company has become complicated over the years. Its beginnings are fairly straightforward. A shareholder puts money into a company and receives shares of stock in return. The complications arise because of the various kinds of stock or stock equivalents that can be issued. For example, there is preferred stock as well as common stock—the difference being that, as the name would indicate, preferred stock is preferred either with regard to a share of the earnings of the company or a prior entitlement to assets upon liquidation, or both. It is a type of equity that, from an economic standpoint, might almost be considered to be a liability. To illustrate this complexity, the following is an example of the explanation of the capital stock section of the balance sheet of the Pollack Corporation.

Pollack Corporation
Statement of Stockholders' Equity
December 31, 1988

9% preferred stock, $50 par value, callable at $55, authorized 20,000 shares, issued and outstanding 12,000 shares.		$ 600,000
Common stock, no par, stated value $2 per share, authorized 500,000 shares, issued 400,000 shares of which 25,000 shares are held in the treasury.		800,000
Additional paid-in capital:		
Preferred	$ 50,000	
Common	1,000,000	1,050,000*

Retained income:

Restricted	$ 500,000	
Unrestricted	1,500,000	2,000,000
Subtotal		$4,450,000
Less: Cost of 25,000 shares of common stock reacquired and held in treasury.		250,000
Total stockholders' equity		$4,200,000

* *Many presentations would not show the detailed breakdown of additional paid-in capital into preferred and common portions. Many presentations would show the restrictions parenthetically, as follows:*

Retained income ($500,000 restricted as to dividends because of loan agreement) $2,000,000.

From a managerial accounting standpoint the capital stock elements of the ownership of a company very often impact most directly on the cost of money to run a division of a company. As indicated earlier, in connection with our discussion in Chapter 4 of the liabilities of a company, these determine what internal cost of money will be charged to a division that needs those resources.

From a tax standpoint, there is a basic issue involved that is very important. If an item is a liability, the interest on it is deductible for tax purposes. If the item is really part of the capital stock of the company (i.e., equity), the payments on that item (i.e., dividends) are not deductible for tax purposes on the corporate tax returns. Consequently, there is much dispute between the IRS and taxpayers as to whether equity is really equity and debt is really debt.

Equally important, regarding the tax implications of the equity section of a balance sheet, is the fact that reorganizations of companies over time have become the fashion in the United States. Large amounts of assets and liabilities are put together in the form of mergers and acquisitions in which shareholders give up shares in their former company and receive shares and other consideration from a new company. The following is a listing of some of the companies regarding which major transactions of this type have taken place over recent years.

American Broadcasting
  Company
American Motors
Bache Halsey Stuart
Beatrice Foods
Bendix
Eastern Airlines
EDS/General Motors
Federated Department
  Stores

Getty Oil
Hughes Tool
E. F. Hutton
KPMG Peat Marwick
People Express
Salomon Brothers
Shearson Lehman
TWA

This listing gives you some feeling for the massive amount of resources that shifted from company to company, whereas the shareholders are really just exchanging pieces of paper. In the minds of the shareholders these transactions are important because they often indicate whether income or loss has resulted. In the case of the company itself, it generally creates a multiplicity of complicated types of common stock, preferred stock, and other stock equivalents that may have to be accounted for in different ways.

ISSUANCE OF SHARES

One of the first considerations in the corporate environment is the issuance, restructuring, and retirement of capital stock of the company. From a financial accounting standpoint, the original issuance of capital stock is reasonably straightforward, although complicated in part by the variety of types of equity documents that a company can issue, as indicated earlier. There are some instruments that have debt as well as equity features. Therefore it becomes a question for financial accounting as to which will prevail and how the instruments should be classified.

Of immediate interest to the corporate executive is what impact these types of instruments have on earnings per share (EPS), the simple formula consisting of the numerator of annual net income of the company and the denominator of the number of shares outstanding. This seems to be a relatively straightforward matter. However, what is the number of shares actually outstanding if a company has issued debt convertible into common stock, debt with options to acquire the stock involved, stock option plans for its employees, and similar transactions that have, as a side issue (although perhaps a major issue), potential for additional shares of stock to be outstanding. In addition, when is preferred stock really preferred and when is it really disguised common stock? The accounting profession has issued a pronouncement dealing with the subject of earnings per share and has concluded that under certain circumstances two earnings-per-share figures are to be issued so that the reader can obtain some feeling for the impact of this complicated area.[1]

One type of earnings per share would be that based on outstanding common stock or what are called common stock equivalents. The other would be a so called "fully diluted" earnings per share, which would take into account what the equity section of the balance sheet would look like if all instruments that could be converted into common stock were indeed converted on the first day of the business year. To get a feeling for this type of situation, study the following comparison between regular and fully diluted earnings per share for Borun Industries, Inc., a company that has a stock option plan for its employees.

Borun Industries, Inc.
COMPUTATION OF EARNINGS PER SHARE

	Primary Earnings Per Share	Fully Diluted Earnings Per Share
Average number of shares under options outstanding	5,000	5,000
Option price per share	× $20	× $20
Proceeds upon exercise of options	100,000	100,000
Market price of common stock:		
Average	$24	
Closing		$28
Treasury shares that could be repurchased with proceeds ($100,000 − $24)	4,166	
($100,000 − $28)		3,571
Excess of shares under option over treasury shares that could be repurchased (5,000 − 4,166)	834	
(5,000 − 3,571)		1,429

Borun Industries, Inc.
COMPUTATION OF EARNINGS PER SHARE (Continued)

Common stock equivalent shares (incremental shares)	834	1,429
Average number of common shares outstanding	100,000	100,000
Total average number of common and common equivalent shares	100,834	101,429
	A	C
Net income for the year	$220,000	$220,000
	B	D
Earnings per share	$2.18 (B÷A)	$2.17 (D÷C)

As can be seen from this exhibit, there are significant financial accounting impacts that result from the innovative financing techniques that have been developed over the years. The financial accounting role has been one of trying to explain to the reader, in some consistent way, what the true equity section of the balance sheet of the company contains.

A little later in this book, when we get to the subject of financial statement analysis in Chapter 8, we shall see that earnings per share is one of the more important indications of the results of a company in the eyes of many financial analysts, professional and amateur. While EPS is only one ratio among many, from a financial statement standpoint, it gives investors one quick indication as to whether they should keep their money in the company or whether they can get a better rate of return elsewhere.

To use a brief illustration, if you can get a relatively risk-free return on an investment at an after-tax rate of, say, 8 percent by investing in an insured certificate of deposit in a banking institution, then earnings per share calculations of a corporation begin to give you some indication as to whether your money in the company is earning a rate of return (after tax) that adequately compensates you for the risk involved in share ownership. The big difference in this illustration is that a certificate of deposit has no growth potential. Indeed, with inflation you would lose a portion of the economic value of your deposit, whereas an investment in a company might give you an opportunity to keep pace with or even exceed inflation in addition to getting a flow of dividends from the stock.

REORGANIZATION

If we go beyond the original issuance of equity instruments and move into reorganizations, we see that the whole area of mergers and acquisitions has been a dynamic one. ("Mergers and acquisitions" is the term used to cover the entire range of activities involved in bringing companies together to form larger business entities, either by having the shareholders of the companies exchange shares and thus continue as owners of the newly formed company or by having some (or all) shareholders bought out.) Since World War II the American economy has experienced the formation of conglomerates, leveraged buyouts, spinoffs of unwanted divisions, and similar major movements among business corporations. (By "conglomerate" is meant a grouping of business operations whose objective is to generate greater profits from the interaction of the various businesses in the group; by "leveraged buyout" is meant a restructuring technique whereby investors (in some cases the company's managers) acquire the company by borrowing funds from third parties. The result is a substitution of debt for equity capital in the operation of the company. By "spin-off" is meant a restructuring whereby a portion of an existing company is transferred to the existing equity owners, who are then able to run the company that has been thus transferred either as a separate business activity apart from the original company or by disposing of the business that has been transferred.) The flexibility provided the business environment during the Reagan Administration enabled much to be done in the consolidation of corporate entities with the lessening degree of concern about the antitrust considerations. What has this meant from an accounting standpoint?

One major series of rules involves the questions of whether an acquisition is a "purchase" or a "pooling of interest." The area of purchase accounting essentially requires that the purchase price for a company be reflected in the redistribution of that price over the underlying assets of the company acquired. This is important from the standpoint of the write-off of the assets and reduction of earnings in the future. The pooling of interest concept, on the other hand, sees a coming together of two companies in a way that would not require the "step-up" in the assets and consequently gives a very different after acquisition accounting treatment. (The term "step-up" is used in accounting to refer to changing the value at which an asset is carried in a company from its original historical cost up to a value that more closely approximates its current fair market value.)

From a tax standpoint mergers and acquisitions (more often called "Subchapter C" issues) involve perhaps the most complicated area of the tax law. (The term "Subchapter C" is the shorthand language used by tax professionals to describe the tax rules dealing with mergers and acquisitions activity. The specific words refer to the portion of the Internal Revenue Code that contains the sections dealing with restructuring issues.) The stakes are high because, if a transaction qualifies as a reorganization, taxpayers are permitted to swap (1) one form of investment in the company for another or (2) one form of investment in the company for that of another company—and not have to pay any tax on the transaction at that point in time.

If a deal does not qualify as a reorganization, then the taxpayer investor can wind up in a position of having exchanged one piece of paper for another but with a tax liability requiring the outlay of cash. Reputations have been made (and lost) by the careful (or not so careful) handling of transactions of this type. One example of this would be a shareholder in Max Factor, the cosmetics company. Years ago the company was acquired by Norton Simon, which was in turn acquired by Esmark, which was in turn acquired by Beatrice Foods. Thus, an investor in Max Factor could wind up with an investment in Beatrice in a series of transactions that would have been tax free.

The basic point about all these restructurings for financial statement purposes is that they change the ownership of a company. It is important that you, as a business person, realize that your interest in an economic entity will change in a merger, buyout or other form of restructuring. For example, a merger may give you a smaller percentage interest of a larger company, whereas the leveraged buyout might give you a larger interest in a group of smaller companies that are created from a larger one. A wise idea therefore is to always make a calculation on a "before and after" tax basis before you enter into transactions of this type, either as an investor or as an owner. From the standpoint of the company itself, these kinds of restructurings need to be explained in the equity section of the balance sheet so that owners (old and new) have a clear idea of where they stand after any restructuring.

From a managerial accounting standpoint these types of restructurings are important to operating people in that it often affects their rate of interest on resources that the treasury department of the company will charge to an operating division. It is not a factor over which internal management at division and department levels have much control. Consequently it is a fact of life that they have to live with. We will see this in greater depth when we get into a later discussion of the use of managerial accounting data in performance measurements of a company. The cost of money resulting from a restructuring of the equity section of a balance sheet will very often not be a variable under the control of division heads and consequently not a matter on which they have a basis of being measured.

From a tax standpoint the major issue is whether a financing instrument is really debt (giving rise to deductible interest expense) or equity (giving rise to nondeductible dividend payments). Simply stated? Yes. Simple to implement? No. Many battles have been fought over the debt versus equity issue from a tax standpoint. Congress tried to settle this problem once and for all with the enactment of Section 385 of the Internal Revenue Code. As part of the tax environment at that time Congress left to the U.S. Treasury Department the job of issuing regulations that would amplify and clarify information on the tax consequences of debt and of equity. After a number of false starts we still do not have regulations because none could be agreed upon between the Treasury Department and the taxpayers making comments on proposed Treasury regulations. Consequently there are no clear guidelines today as to when equity exists and when debt exists from the standpoint of the tax law.

To give the reader some feeling for the measures that are used to determine when debt or equity exists under the Internal Revenue Code, the following are the guidelines that are spelled out in Section 385:

1. Is there a written, unconditional promise to pay on demand or on a specified date a sum certain in money in return for an adequate consideration in money's worth and to pay a fixed rate of interest?
2. Is there any subordination to or preference over any other indebtedness of the corporation?
3. What is the ratio of debt to equity of the corporation?
4. Is there any convertibility of the debt into stock of the company?
5. What is the relationship between the holdings of stock in the corporation and the holdings of the debt in question?

From a tax accounting standpoint the restructuring of companies is an extremely complicated area. This can be made simple for the reader of this book by realizing that, if you give up pieces of paper (shares) in company A and receive pieces of paper in company B as a result of a merger, you may have a paper gain but you do not have cash with which to pay any tax that might be due on that gain. Consequently, the tax law provides mechanisms for treating such transactions, even very large ones, in a way that allows the taxpayer to defer the payment of tax until the shares of company B in this illustration are ultimately disposed of in return for cash or for some asset that is a cash equivalent. In addition, the companies themselves that are restructured are not new companies but are really a reorganization of existing companies. The tax law here also allows major restructuring to be performed in a way that permits the assets and liabilities to move forward as if no taxable transaction had taken place. In the heydays of the 1960s many tax-free reorganizations took place, with the net result that tax payment was pushed forward to future periods. This made tax accounting an important part of the equation in these kinds of transactions.

In recent days many of the reorganizations have had cash involved and, as a result, could not qualify for tax-free treatment. Of course, with a receipt of cash the shareholders as well as the corporation had the wherewithal to pay tax liabilities. The basic idea to keep in mind here is that the tax law requires that, when transactions take place, the general rule is that the fair market value of what you receive over the cost (called "Tax Basis") of what you gave up is taxable unless you can locate a provision of the Internal Revenue Code that makes it tax free and not vice versa.

Because of the involvement of the corporate side of the organization, operating divisions would probably not have much concern from a managerial accounting standpoint with regard to these types of reorganizations. Once again, however, the cost of money that would be charged to the operating divisions can be impacted by corporate reorganizations. Managerial accounting does come into play, however, after a company has been split up as part of a reorganization. This is because the various pieces of the former company must now be measured as if they were separate companies. Managerial accounting is used to record the separation not only of the assets and liabilities of the former company into their various components but also of its income and expense.

Chapter 6 will treat the subject of the income and expense items that enter into the accounting for a company. Suffice it to say at this point that once a company is reorganized into various portions, managerial accounting is crucial in determining what items of income and expense belong in the various divisions.

RETAINED EARNINGS

Remember that the equity section of a balance sheet includes the accumulation of earnings from a series of periods, at least to the extent they have not been paid out as dividends over that period. Therefore, from an accounting standpoint the term *retained earnings* means the net income from a given year less dividends paid out over time. The statement of retained earnings is the bridge between the income statement (discussed in Chapter 6) and the balance sheet (discussed in Chapters 2-5). What real significance has the statement of retained earnings?

The big issue to the business person really is what items belong in the income statement and what items belong in the statement of retained earnings. In the past there have been two schools of thought with regard to this issue. One school said that the income statement should only contain those items relating to the continuing operations of the company and that the statement of retained earnings should contain everything else that would be extraneous in nature. The other school said exactly the opposite. That is, put everything into the income statement and leave the statement of retained earnings to include only the net income on an "all-inclusive" basis, less dividends declared and paid.

From a financial accounting standpoint there is a fairly simple financial statement, the Statement of Changes in Retained Earnings, which is a bridge between the balance sheet and the income statement. As we will see in Chapter 6, an income statement basically takes the income that a company earns, subtracts the expenses, and produces a net income or loss figure (which is the difference). That net income figure can be paid to the owner of the business in the form of dividends (if it is a corporation). However, in most businesses the entire net income for the year is not paid in dividends. Rather, some of the net income is "retained" by the company for future expansion. Indeed, if shareholders think that investing in the company is a good deal, what they are really thinking is they can get a better rate of return from the company than from some alternative investment. Consequently, they would want the company to retain some of those earnings. Thus, when net income is $100 and dividend payout is $50, the $50 that is left is called retained earnings. It is accumulated over the years and becomes part of the equity section of the balance sheet. Therefore, the statement of retained earnings in simplified form looks as follows:

Retained earnings January 1, 1989	$1,000
plus Net income for the year	+ 100
minus Dividends paid during the year	− 50
equals Retained earnings December 31, 1989	$1,050

This last figure (retained earnings at the year-end), when added to the capital stock of a company, constitutes the equity section of a balance sheet. From the standpoint of financial statement analysis, this gives some figures to use in making further evaluation of the company. For example, if the company has $1,000 of stock outstanding, the dividend payout ratio would be $50 dividend over $1,000, or 5 percent. An investor who looked closely at the company's increase in value of the shares over the years might be satisfied with a payout ratio of this amount. On the other hand, senior citizens who are dependent on current cash for their finances might feel a ratio of this type to be inadequate and would therefore shift their investment to companies that have a higher dividend payout ratio.

To give you an overview of what we have seen to this point, you should review the following schematic:

THE BALANCE SHEET SCHEMATIC

ASSETS	MINUS	LIABILITIES	EQUALS	OWNER'S EQUITY
Chapters 2 & 3		Chapter 4		Chapter 5

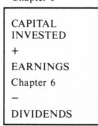

CAPITAL
INVESTED
+
EARNINGS
Chapter 6
−
DIVIDENDS

CHAPTER PERSPECTIVE

In this chapter we have completed our coverage of the contents of the balance sheet, consisting of assets, liabilities, and ownership in the company. From this, the average businessperson should have a feeling for the major elements that go into each one of those categories and how they interrelate.

We have gained an appreciation of how the accounting and tax requirements impact the issuance of shares to create a company. We have also seen how a company's ownership is impacted by the accumulation of earnings from year to year and how its performance is measured on an annual basis by the computation of earnings per share.

We have also gained an appreciation of how the accounting rules treat the restructuring of organizations, particularly in the mergers and acquisitions area, which has become an important part of American business.

Finally, we have seen that accounting and taxation rules come to play not only in the combining of companies but also in the divestiture of companies. Having now acquired a foundation for looking at a company at a point in time, we will move into Chapter 6, which will help us gain an appreciation of how accounting and taxation rules are impacted by the annual activities of a company.

FOOTNOTES

1 *"Accounting For Earnings Per Share" Opinion of the Accounting Principles Board No. 15 (New York: AICPA, 1969).*

The Income Statement: Are We Making Money?

INTRODUCTION AND MAIN POINTS

In previous chapters we have concentrated on the balance sheet. Now we will look at the financial statement that reflects the activities that take place over a period of time. In essence, it is part of the answer to the question, "Are we making money?"

In this chapter we will focus on the various elements of income and expense that constitute the income statement. We will concentrate on how these activities interrelate with the assets and liabilities that we discussed on the balance sheet, so that we have an overall appreciation for the accounting for these transactions.

In addition, we will look at certain major areas of income statements with particular emphasis on those areas that have complicated accounting and taxation rules—namely, leasing, pensions, income taxes, franchising, and contract manufacturing. We will also have an opportunity of gaining an appreciation for the variety of types of items that go into the classifications in an income statement, with particular emphasis being placed on activities that are not part of the ordinary operations of the company for the year in question.

After studying the material in this chapter:

▬ You will understand the importance of the income statement.

▬ You will know the format of the transaction approach to the income statement.

▬ You will know how to use an income statement to determine the financial health of a business.

▬ You will see how leasing fits into the overall income picture.

▬ You will understand how tax items are handled on the income statement.

IMPORTANCE

Over the years the income statement has become the statement of greatest interest to investors and companies. It is the statement that measures results for a period of time (usually one year) and is a measure of the performance of the management of the company running it. Coupled with a balance sheet, the income statement gives the reader an opportunity to see where a company is at a given point in time and also what the company has done over the past year. Adding the statement of retained earnings mentioned in Chapter 5 provides the reader with the means to evaluate not only where the company was at the beginning of the year but also what happened during that year and where the company stands at the end of the year.

The importance of a statement of income is that it gives the reader an opportunity of seeing whether the activity was profitable during the year. It also gives some hints as to the extent to which cash flows are going into and out of the company, and thus gives an idea of whether or not the company is in a position to have the resources it needs to cover debt obligations as well as to return cash to the owners. The disadvantage of the income statement is that it does not include many of the items that contribute to the general growth and well-being of an enterprise because of accounting's conventions that have been adopted. For example, one company might choose to depreciate its plant assets on an accelerated basis, while another may choose a straight-line basis. The ability to compare these companies then becomes more difficult because one may seem to have not had as good a year financially as the other by showing a lower net income. The reader, given more information, would see that they may have performed equally over the year. In essence, this information is important from the standpoint of knowing the quality of earnings, as well as the quantity of earnings, for a given enterprise.

FORMAT

While an income statement might be put together by just taking (1) the value of assets minus liabilities at the end of the year and subtracting (2) the same number at the beginning of the year and (3) using this net approach to determine what went on in the company, financial accounting does not adopt this "capital change" approach. Rather it uses what is called a "transaction" approach. It is not important for the reader to understand this terminology beyond the fact that the transaction approach measures the basic income-related transactions that occurred during a period and summarizes them in an income statement. This approach focuses on the activities that have occurred during the year or another period of time and discloses the components that comprise the change.

In sum, an income statement totals up all the sources of revenue (such as sales of products, fees for services, leasing of realty, licensing intangible assets, rental income for leasing tangible assets) and subtracts the expenses related to them (such as the cost of the acquiring or manufacturing of goods that are sold, compensation of the people rendering the services, and the cost of administering the company, including the interest expenses on funds borrowed as well as the cost of research and development).

There are also many types of gains or losses such as those resulting from the sale of investments, the sale of fixed assets, the settlement of liabilities, and the write-off of assets due to obsolescence or casualty and theft.

Set forth below is a simplified version of an income statement that includes all the essential ingredients.

Simplified Income Statement

Sales		175
Less returns and allowances		25
Net sales		150
Less Cost of Goods Sold:		
Beginning inventory	100	
Purchases	50	
	150	
Ending inventory	50	
		100
Gross profit		50
Less selling and administrative expenses		25
Net income		25

At this point let's "walk through" this example income statement and see how it would interrelate with items on the balance sheet. In the case of net sales revenue, a company would sell its products and would generally either receive cash, which would be reflected on the balance sheet, or, more often, receive an account receivable from the customer, thus relating to that item on the balance sheet. In the case of cost of goods sold section, this is comprised of taking the inventory on hand at the beginning of the year, adding to it whatever purchases were made during the year (giving a figure for the cost of goods available for sale), and then subtracting the inventory at the end of the year. In this example the cost of goods actually sold is $100. It would not be appropriate to report that the business made a net income of $100 and forget the fact that it cost $50 to sell that product.

Similarly, if the company is a service organization, it would not be appropriate to show as net income the fees received for services rendered to clients without taking into account the salaries paid to the people rendering the services.

Sounds simple enough, but it's not. For example, there are variations of the times at which income can be recognized from the sale of products. Normally that recognition takes place when all of the requirements are fulfilled for passing title of merchandise to the customer. However, in those situations where there are long-term contracts that might take several years to complete, the financial accounting convention permits the company either to wait until the contract is completed to record the income or to record it on a percentage basis in connection with the state of completion of the project. Thus, long-term contracts have their own rules. An example of the long-term contract type of accounting would be one in which Stewart Construction Company decides to reports its income during the period the contract is still being fulfilled, as opposed to waiting until the end of the contact to report the income.

STEWART CONSTRUCTION COMPANY

	1986	1987	1988
Contract price	$ 4,500,000	$ 4,500,000	$ 4,500,000
Less estimated cost:			
Costs to date	1,000,000	2,916,000	4,050,000
Estimated cost to complete	3,000,000	1,134,000	—
Estimated total costs	4,000,000	4,050,000	4,050,000
Estimated total gross profit	$ 500,000	$ 450,000	$ 450,000
Percent complete:	25%	72%	100%
	($1,000,000)	($2,916,000)	($4,050,000)
	($4,000,000)	($4,050,000)	($4,050,000)

To illustrate the installment method in accounting for the sales of merchandise, we can assume the following information:

	1986	1987	1988
Sales (on installment)	$ 200,000	$ 250,000	$ 240,000
Cost of sales	150,000	190,000	168,000
Gross profit	$ 50,000	$ 60,000	$ 72,000
Rate of gross profit on sales	25%[a]	24%[b]	30%[c]
Cash receipts			
1986 sales	$ 60,000	$ 100,000	$ 40,000
1987 sales		100,000	125,000
1988 sales			80,000

[a] $ 50,000	[b] $ 60,000	[c] $ 72,000
$200,000	$250,000	$240,000

In situations of this type, income is not recorded until cash payments are actually received. In essence, this involves computing the ratio of gross profit on the sales to total sales and using that percentage of cash receipts to record the income.

Therefore, where products are sold on an installment basis, it may be appropriate to record the income at the time of the sale, even though all the payments haven't yet been made; or else defer the gain and record it piecemeal as collections are made. However, in some instances where the creditworthiness of the customer is in question and it is not certain that all the cash will be received, it may be more appropriate to record the income on a cost recovery method whereby income is only recognized after enough cash is received to at least recover the cost of the product sold.

FRANCHISING

As the United States has moved into a service economy status, accounting for service income also gets complicated. For example, franchising is an activity in which a number of elements come into question when income is to be recorded. It starts with the sale of the franchise itself. It is complicated by continuing franchise fees that have to be paid. It continues through the phase where the franchisee might have an option to purchase the franchise. Finally, it involves the calculation of the costs of the franchiser as well as the franchisee in determining whether the operation has produced a profit or a loss.

CONTRACT MANUFACTURING

Another complex area is one of contract manufacturing. This is becoming a common practice these days of high-tech companies, where a business person may have an idea for a new product but does not have the facilities for actually manufacturing it. This activity would be contracted out to some other company. Again, at what point in time is it appropriate to match off (1) the revenues from selling the product with (2) the research and development costs that have been incurred to come up with the idea for the product, as well as (3) the production costs involved with purchasing the raw materials and the cost of labor as well as (4) the financing costs for carrying accounts receivable from the customers purchasing the final product?

LEASING

An additional area in which the financial accounting rules for treatment of transactions get complicated is the area of leasing. In the days when a lease was a lease, one party owned an asset and rented it to another party. Many people have experienced this when they go to Hertz to rent a car. Hertz owns the car, rents it to us, we drive it for several days, return the car to Hertz, and pay them a fee for that service.

Over time, however, companies have found that leasing can be an interesting way to have the opportunity to utilize assets they need for their business without having to reflect either the ownership of the assets on their books or, even more importantly, having to show the liabilities involved with the purchase of the asset. The answer has been leasing.

Let us examine a simple illustration. Suppose the company needs a particular piece of machinery that costs $1,000,000. In order to have the use of that asset they could borrow $1,000,000 with interest at 10 percent and then go out and purchase the asset. The balance sheet effect would be to show an asset of $1,000,000 and a liability of $1,000,000. The expenses related to that transaction would be twofold: the depreciation of the asset—that is, spreading the cost of the asset over its useful life on some systematic basis—and the interest cost on the liability incurred.

However, some companies have reached the point where liabilities on their balance sheet are so large that they have gotten warnings from their lenders that they are reaching the limits of their borrowing capacity. What do they do about this dilemma? On the one hand, the company needs the asset for its business; on the other hand, it is restricted in borrowing more money to purchase the asset. The answer is leasing. What happens is the company goes to the party that owns the asset and says, "We cannot afford to buy it, but can we rent it?" A deal is then worked out whereby the company has the use of the asset for a period of time during which the rental payments would be recorded as an expense. Thus, there would not be depreciation and interest costs, only rental payments.

As a result of this situation, a whole new industry has developed involving not only the manufacture of the product as the lessor, but also a middle man who would buy the asset from the manufacturer and, in turn, would lease to the user. A perfect example of this is found in the sale or lease of large equipment such as airplanes, sophisticated manufacturing equipment, fleets of automobiles and trucks, and, indeed, almost anything you can think of in terms of assets needed in a business.

The accounting for this is quite complex. Suffice it to say at this point that accounting rules require that the transaction be analyzed to see whether it is, in fact, a lease or just a disguised purchase. This involves looking at the period of time over which the lease agreement is in effect, the payments being made during the lease, whether the person renting the equipment has the ability to make a bargain purchase at the end of the lease (i.e., acquire the equipment for a nominal amount), and items of a similar nature involving the basic economics of the transaction.

Assume a situation where an agreement involves leasing the asset for, in effect, its entire useful life, with the lessee making payments that are, in effect, the equivalent of what the interest cost of borrowing as well as the servicing of the payments of the principal on the debt would be, but having the right to buy the equipment at a nominal price at the end of the lease. All this would add up to what would be considered in reality a purchase and would have to be reflected on the balance sheet as if a purchase had been made. The saying would be "if it looks like a duck and walks like a duck and quacks like a duck, it's not an eagle—it's a duck," so treat it that way from an accounting standpoint.

RETIREMENT OBLIGATIONS

Another area of major controversy in accounting deals with pensions and other retirement obligations a company has to its employees. Billions of dollars are involved in this issue. Essentially the question is whether or not a company can reduce its net income by reflecting the expense it is incurring to provide retirement benefits for its employees. For many years companies have simply recorded the amount of cash they actually had to pay to those people who were retired. But some analysts have warned that this does not appropriately match income and expenses because current employees are building up future pension costs for the company, and those costs have not been matched off against the profit of the company in the current year. In other words, the retired employees worked to make the profits of prior years, and the current employees are making the sales and service income of current years.

Once again we are dealing with a subject of tremendous complication because of the actual calculations that are needed to determine what amount might have to be set aside in the current year for people who have not yet begun to collect pension benefits. How do you factor into the equation the workers of today who will not qualify for pension benefit because they will leave the company before they are "vested" in the plan ("vesting" means that the person has been employed long enough and has reached a sufficient age to have earned a pension, which, if they left the company, would have to be paid out to them in cash). The current mobility of workers presents a situation where, in many cases, an expense could be recorded and a liability put on the balance sheet for amounts that would never have to be paid. Similarly, where a company does not set aside actual cash to fund these plans, consideration would have to be given to the income that those investments would earn. This is fraught with controversy. At the present time the accounting standards require only that some minimum liability amount be reflected in the financial statements, given the obligations that will have to be paid in the future related to the pension plans.

To illustrate, below is a footnote from a financial statement of the Johnson & Johnson Company that explains in a fair amount of detail the elements of what we are discussing. The important thing to remember is that the area is complicated, the accounting treatment is unsettled, substantial amounts of money are involved, and it is a major area where matching of expenses to revenue could produce significantly different results, depending on how pension funds are accounted for.

The Company has various retirement and pension plans which cover substantially all employees of its domestic operations. Most international subsidiaries also have retirement plans. Total pension expense related to these plans amounted to $44.2 million in 1986, $51.6 million in 1985 and $57.4 million in 1984. In 1985 the Company adopted, with respect to its domestic pension plans, Statement of Financial Accounting Standards (FAS) No. 87, Employer's Accounting for Pensions, which supersedes all previous standards for pension accounting. The effect of the adoption of FAS No. 87, in part offset by certain plan benefit improvements, reduced 1985 pension expense by $11.8 million.

The domestic plan benefits are primarily based on the employee's compensation during the five years before retirement and the number of years service. The Company's objective in funding its plans is to accumulate funds sufficient to provide for all accrued benefits and to maintain a relatively stable contribution level in the future. Net pension expense for the domestic plans for 1986 and 1985 included the following components (in millions):

	1986	1985
Service cost-benefits earned during period	$ 33.9	$ 32.2
Interest cost on projected benefit obligations	54.1	49.0
Actual return on assets	(121.9)	(171.4)
Net amortization and deferral	60.6	117.3
Curtailment gain-credited to redirection charges	$ (17.2)	—
Net periodic pension cost	$ 9.5	$ 27.1

The domestic plans are fully funded. The following table sets forth the actuarial present value of benefit obligations and funded status at December 31, 1986 and 1985 for the Company's domestic plans (in millions):

Accumulated benefit obligations, including vested benefits of $483.2 ($388.8 in 1985)	$ 518.0	$ 417.4
Plan assets at fair value, primarily stocks and bonds	$ 903.7	$ 801.0
Unrecognized prior service cost	2.0	
Less:		
Projected benefit obligations	764.0	600.2
Unrecognized net gain on assets	76.7	123.0
Unamortized net assets at January 1, 1985	69.8	75.6
Net pension (liabilities) assets	$ (4.8)	$ 2.2

The expected long-term rate of return on plan assets was 8.5% for 1986 and 1985 and 8.0-8.5% for 1984. The weighted average discount rates for 1986 and 1985 were 8% and 9%, respectively. The rate of increase in future compensation levels used in determining the actuarial present value of accumulated benefit obligations for 1986 and 1985 was 7.5%.

International subsidiaries have plans under which funds are deposited with trustees, annuities are purchased under group contracts, or reserves are provided. It is estimated that the market value of fund assets and reserves of individual international subsidiaries exceeded or approximated the actuarial present value of accumulated benefits at January 1, 1986 and January 1, 1985.

INCOME TAXES

A final area of controversy in income statements is that of accounting for income taxes. As we discussed in Chapter 4, a company may adopt tax accounting rules that differ from standard financial and managerial accounting rules. For example, one firm might record income from installment sales for financial accounting purposes by taking into income all the profit at the time of the sales, but for tax purposes the firm would report the income only over the period of time when the installment payments were received. In addition, in the case of long-term contracts, companies might decide to report for financial accounting purposes the profit as a long-term project was being worked on, whereas for tax purposes such companies would only report the income when all work was done. We have also seen that it is possible to use a straight line method for the depreciation of assets for financial statement purposes and accelerated methods of depreciation for tax purposes.

How are these tax items handled for accounting purposes? There are two basic theories involved. One is that, in recording an income tax expense in any year, you look at what you actually owe the Internal Revenue Service and that is your expense. The fact that it might be much less (or much more) than the tax that would be due if you used your accounting income as if it were taxable income, is not taken into account.

Another basic method that is utilized is called a "deferral method." Using this method you pretend that your accounting income is really your taxable income, so you compute your income tax expense on an "as if" basis. The Financial Accounting Standards Board has reviewed this matter and came to the conclusion that the deferral system, which has been in effect until recent years, should change to a so-called liability method.

The basic significance of this is that, instead of giving primary emphasis to the income tax expense on the income statement by using the deferral income method, more emphasis is given to the income tax liability on the balance sheet. Consequently, the accounting standard of the future would be one that emphasizes the question, "Does the liability you are showing on your balance sheet closely approximate what you are actually going to have to pay in tax?" The fact that the income tax expense in the income statement bears no logical relationship to the net income before taxes for accounting purposes, would be de-emphasized for financial statement analysis purposes. It is important to realize that, by looking at an income statement in the future, it will be harder to ascertain whether the reason the company is showing net income after taxes at a higher rate is due to a better performance in that year or just because management has been able to drive down its income expense in the current year by adopting accounting methods that will push into the future the payment of those tax amounts.

Set forth below is a simple comparison of how differences of this type will bring about different results and considerations that will have to be taken into account in evaluating the result of the company activities.

	Financial Statements	Tax Return
Net income before depreciation	100,000	100,000
Depreciation	30,000	50,000
Net income	70,000	50,000
Tax rate	40%	40%
Tax	28,000	20,000

WHAT IS NET INCOME?

You must feel at this point that the complexities in this area have reached their highest point. Unfortunately, that is not true. We pointed out earlier that in addition to the income statement, there is a statement of retained earnings. As these earnings accumulate year after year, they are measured by an entry on the balance sheet called Retained Earnings. In the past it was considered important that emphasis be given to show in the income statement only the revenue and expenses related to the current operations of a company. Indeed, the name of that method is called the "current operating performance" approach. This puts in the income statement only those items that relate to continuing operations and puts everything else in the statement of retained earnings.

Over time, however, a philosophy has arisen that favors the opposite direction. That is, put in the income statement almost everything and restrict the number of items going into the retained earnings statement. This gives the reader as comprehensive a view as possible of everything that went on (plus or minus) during the current year. This is called the "all-inclusive income approach." The financial accounting convention that has been adopted is the second one. Consequently, since the type of income and expense that go into an income statement will vary in quality, that factor requires items to be set out separately such as

(1) extraordinary items, (2) unusual gains and losses, (3) prior period adjustments, (4) changes in accounting principles, and (5) discontinued operations. Let's see what these items mean.

Extraordinary items are considered to be those types of income or expense that are unusual in nature and do not occur very frequently. For example, this would be the situation resulting from the billions of dollars in losses incurred by companies as a result of the California earthquakes and East Coast hurricanes. The conclusion with these types of items is that they are to be reflected separately in the income statement, net of the income tax amount related to them. (Net of income tax is a phrase in the income statement that means that the figure is a net figure, after having subtracted the amount of income tax attributed to that item).

Unusual gains and losses are items that are either unusual in nature or happen infrequently, but not both. An example of this would be a situation where one company might acquire another for a purchase price based on values in excess of the book value of assets shown on the balance sheet of the acquired company. If management feels that these assets no longer have significant value, they will write the assets down. In this particular case the write-down is shown in the income statement—together with other income and expenses—but not on a net-after-tax basis. The difference between this category and extraordinary items mentioned above is that the result would be part of the net income from continuing operations.

What about *prior period adjustments*? These are situations where a company finds out that it made an incorrect recording of an item in a prior period. For example, suppose a company determines that it overstated its depreciation expense in an early year. This error would have affected both the income statement and the tax return for the prior year, which now have to be corrected. Here is one of the few areas where an item is allowed to be reflected in the statement of retained earnings and not the income statement. Thus, it does not enter into net income in the current year at all, but rather is reflected in the statement of retained earnings.

In connection with the *changes in accounting principles*, suppose the company decided to change its method of inventory costing from the first-in, first-out method (FIFO) to the last-in, first-out method (LIFO), or that it is going to change its depreciation method from a declining balance to a straight-line method. These types of changes are recognized in financial accounting by including them in the income statement of the current year net of tax related to them. The effect on net income of adopting the new accounting principle would be to show it as a separate item on the income statement following the recording of any extraordinary items of a type described above.

Finally, what about the item labeled *discontinued operations*? This has been extensively used in recent years as companies coming through the acquisition surge of the 1960s have found that some businesses are not compatible with their overall operations and no longer fit into the strategies of the firm. A good example of this is found in the Libresco Industries Income Statement for the year ending December 31, 1986.

LIBRESCO INDUSTRIES, INC.
INCOME STATEMENT
FOR THE YEAR ENDED DECEMBER 31, 1986

Sales revenue		$1,480,000
Cost of goods sold		600,000
Gross profit		880,000
Selling and administrative expenses		320,000
Income from operations		560,000
Other revenues and gains		
Interest revenue		10,000
Other expenses and losses		
Loss on disposal of part of Steel Division	$ (5,000)	
Unusual charge—loss on sale of investments	(45,000)	(50,000)
Income from continuing operation before income taxes		520,000
Income taxes		208,000
Income from continuing operations		$ 312,000
Discontinued operations		
Income from operations of Hartley Division, less applicable income taxes of $36,000	54,000	
Loss on disposal of Hartley Division, less applicable income taxes of $60,000	(90,000)	(36,000)
Income before extraordinary item and cumulative effect of accounting change		276,000
Extraordinary item—loss from earthquake, less applicable income taxes of $30,000		(45,000)
Cumulative effect in prior years of retroactive application of new depreciation method, less applicable income taxes of $40,000		(60,000)
Net income		$ 171,000

Per share of common stock
Income from continuing operations . . . . . .   \$ 3.12
Income from operations of discontinued
     division, net of tax 54
Loss on disposal of discontinued operation, net
     of tax . . . .   (.90)

Income before extraordinary item and
     cumulative effect 2.76
Extraordinary loss net of tax . . . .   (.45)
Cumulative effect of change in accounting
     principle, net of tax . . . .   (.60)

Net income . . . .   \$ 1.71

Discontinued operations therefore are another separate income statement category, not only for the gain or loss resulting from disposal of a segment of a business, but also for the result of operations of a segment that has been (or will be) discontinued.

In order to see how all these things interrelate, peruse Table 6-1 which sets out a comparison of how these various types of situations are treated and the criteria that apply to determine whether they exist.

TABLE 6-1

Summary of ABP Opinions and FASB Standards

Type of Situation	Criteria	Examples	Placement on Financial Statements
Extraordinary items	Material, and both unusual and infrequent (non-recurring).	Gains or losses resulting from casualties, an ex-propriation, or a prohibition under a new law.	Separate section in the income statement entitled extraordinary items. (Shown net of tax)
Unusual gains or losses, not considered extraordinary	Material; character typical of the customary business activities; unusual or infrequent but not both.	Write-downs of receivables, inventories; adjustments of accrued contract prices; gains or losses from fluctuations of foreign exchange; gains or losses from sales of assets used in business.	Separate section in income statement above income before extraordinary items. Often reported in other revenues and gains or other expenses and losses section. (Not shown net of tax)

Continued on the following page

Type of Situation	Criteria	Examples	Placement on Financial Statements
Prior period adjustments and accounting changes that require restatement	Material corrections of errors applicable to prior periods or accounting changes required or permitted by an FASB Statement or an APB Opinion to be handled retroactively.	Correction of errors; retroactive restatement per APB Opinion No. 20 or other authoritative pronouncements.	Adjust the beginning balance of retained earnings. (Shown net of tax)
Changes in estimates	Normal, recurring corrections and adjustments.	Changes in the realizability of receivables and inventories; changes in estimated lives of equipment, intangible assets; changes in estimated liability for warranty costs, income taxes, and salary payments.	Change in income statement only in the account affected. (Not shown net of tax)
Changes in principle	Change from one generally accepted principle to another.	Changing the basis of inventory pricing from FIFO to average cost; change in the method of depreciation from accelerated to straightline.	Cumulative effect of the adjustment is reflected in the income statement between the captions extraordinary items and net income. (Shown net of tax)
Discontinued operations	Disposal of a segment of a business constituting a separate line of business or class of customer.	Sale by diversified company of major division that represents only activities in electronics industry. Food distributor that sells wholesale to supermarket chains and through fast-food restaurants decides to discontinue the division that sells to one of two classes of customers.	Shown in separate section of the income statement after continuing operations but before extraordinary items. (Shown net of tax)

Is this complicated? You bet it is! But again the goal is not to make the reader of the financial statement an expert in these various categories. Rather, it is a matter of ascertaining how a business person can properly evaluate what has been going on in the company. It may well be that a company looks like it has had a poor year when all it did was bite the bullet on poor operations and take a one-time hit.

In order to evaluate a company in this situation, the reader should focus on the income or loss from *continuing* operations, which reflect what is going to happen on a forward basis. It may also be telling people where extraordinary items have crept into the activity, that these may very likely not happen in the future and consequently should be taken into account in evaluating the performance of management.

For the reasons expressed above, the earnings-per-share calculations of a company are also generally performed by setting out not just a single figure but also many figures that take into account these particular types of items. Where a company has several different types of earnings— ordinary income, extraordinary items, discontinued operations, etc.—the earnings per share may be calculated for each of these individual types of net income. To illustrate this, set out below is an example of a calculation that reflects not only the earnings per share from continuing operations but also the earnings per share implications for extraordinary items, unusual gains and losses, and discontinued operations.

LIBRESCO INDUSTRIES, INC.

Per share of common stock:

Income from continuing operations	$ 3.12
Income from operation, discontinued division, net of tax	.54
Loss on disposal of discontinued operations, net of tax	(.90)
Income before extraordinary item and cumulative effect	$ 2.76
Extraordinary loss, net of tax	(.45)
Cumulative effect of change in accounting principle, net of tax	(.60)
Net income	$ 1.71

Suppose that in the industry of which Libresco is a part, the normal ratio of the price of stock to net income is 10:1: Would you buy stock in this company? If you look only at the earnings per share on net income after all unusual items, you might decide no. On the other hand, if you looked at earnings per share for continuing operations, you might say, Yes it's a great buy, because on a going-forward basis at a 10:1 price/earnings ratio this company is underpriced. It is considerations of this type that make an understanding of the income statement elements discussed in this chapter so important.

CHAPTER PERSPECTIVE

In this chapter we have analyzed and explained one of the most important financial statements, the income statement. We have seen that it gives a picture of what has happened to the company during the current year. We now have a glimpse of the way in which sales and expenses of a company are reflected in income statements. We also have seen how an income statement is refined by showing not only earnings generated from ordinary operations in a given year, but also unusual transactions that crop up during the year. We have also now had a glimpse of particular types of complicated accounting for such items as franchising, pensions, leasing, and income taxes. Finally, we have obtained a preliminary understanding of earnings per share and how that figure is used in an evaluation of a company in comparison with its competitors.

Statement of Changes in Financial Position and Cash Flow

INTRODUCTION AND MAIN POINTS

In this chapter we will look at a different type of financial statement, namely one that enables a business person to evaluate what has been going on within a company during the past year from a different perspective than is offered by the income statement. We will look at the way in which cash flows through a company as opposed to the way in which net income is computed in a normal income statement. The statement of change in cash flow is useful to the entrepreneur as well as the business manager of a segment of a company. In this chapter we will focus on the cash flow statement as a business-management technique.

After studying the material in this chapter:

■ You will be able to evaluate how cash comes into a company through the normal operations during the year.

■ You will understand how cash comes into the company by the incurring of new debt obligations.

■ You will be able to evaluate the manner in which cash is provided by issuing additional shares of stock of the company and other equity instruments issued by the company.

■ You will see how cash is utilized in the acquisition of new assets as well as the acquisition of new companies.

■ You will see how cash is utilized in paying off debt to creditors as well as paying dividends to shareholders.

To this point we have discussed the balance sheet, the income statement, and the statement of retained earnings. These statements have told us, in effect, what the company looks like at a particular point in time (the balance sheet), what the company has done over the past year (the income statement), and what the effects have been on the net income statement after payment of dividends to the shareholders (statement of retained earnings). Are there any other financial statements we should know about? The answer is yes, the statement of changes in financial position.

We have often been struck by the fact that a business person who looked at the three basic statements mentioned above might logically conclude that they did not give the reader the ability to see what has been going on in the company. Looking at it from a different angle, it is not that the net income statement doesn't tell us about the income and expenses. It does, but it does not tell about the flow of resources into and out of the company. We can therefore envision a "street-smart" business person taking the balance sheets at the beginning of the year and the end of the year, putting them side by side, and just running his or her eye back and forth between the amount of cash at the beginning and the end of the year, the accounts receivable at the beginning and end of the year, the inventories at the beginning and end of the year, etc., in order to get a feeling for how funds came into and left the company. But it is not necessary to go through this time-consuming process, because there is a fairly sophisticated financial statement that does this on a more organized basis.

When the statement of changes in financial position first emerged, essentially it was viewed as looking at what caused the difference in the changes in "working capital." ("Working capital," in essence, is current assets—see Chapter 2—minus current liabilities—see Chapter 4. Any transaction that increased or decreased working capital was shown in this statement. For example, the purchase of equipment for cash or on short-term credit would be reported in the changes statement because it resulted in a change in working capital. The utilization of cash to retire long-term debt that was outstanding is, another change that required the use of working capital.

(A simple illustration of how this would occur is set forth in the report on the next page from the Wharton Company.)

Over time, however, companies have paid much more attention to the cash flow of a company. Under this concept the changes in the cash balance that occurred over a period of time are analyzed. This in effect says, Don't just look at the net changes in working capital—look at the net changes in cash.

WHARTON COMPANY
STATEMENT OF CHANGES IN FINANCIAL POSITION
FOR THE YEAR ENDED DECEMBER 31, 1987

Resources provided by Operations:		
Net income		$19,600
Add (or deduct) items not affecting working capital		
Gain on sale of land	$(1,000)	
Depreciation expense	6,500	5,500
Working capital provided by operations		$25,100
Sale of land		7,000
Sale of equipment		1,500
Issuance of bonds payable		7,500
Total resources provided		$41,100
Resources applied to		
Cash dividends	11,000	
Purchase of equipment	40,000	
Total resources applied		51,000
Decrease in working capital		$ 9,900

SCHEDULE OF WORKING CAPITAL CHANGES

	Working Capital Change	
	Increase	*Decrease*
Current assets		
Increase in cash	1,600	
Decrease in accounts receivable (net)		$ 3,700
Decrease in inventories		13,500
Increase in prepaid expenses	200	
Current liabilities		
Decrease in accounts payable	5,500	
	7,300	17,200
Decrease in working capital	9,900	
	$17,200	$17,200

A comparison with the changes in working capital in this regard is illustrated by the following example.

ADVERTISING CONSULTANTS INC.
COMPARATIVE BALANCE SHEET
DECEMBER 31

Assets	1989	1988	Change Increase/Decrease
Cash	$ 37,000	$49,000	$ 12,000 Decrease
Accounts receivable	26,000	$36,000	10,000 Decrease
Prepaid expenses	6,000	-0-	6,000 Increase
Land	70,000	-0-	70,000 Increase
Building	200,000	-0-	200,000 Increase
Accumulated depreciation—building	(11,000)	-0-	11,000 Increase
Equipment	68,000	-0-	68,000 Increase
Accumulated depreciation—equipment	(10,000)	-0-	10,000 Increase
Total	$386,000	$85,000	

Liabilities and Stockholders' Equity			
Accounts payable	$ 40,000	$ 5,000	35,000 Increase
Bonds payable	150,000	-0-	150,000 Increase
Common stock	60,000	60,000	-0-
Retained earnings	136,000	20,000	116,000 Increase
	$386,000	$85,000	

ADVERTISING CONSULTANTS INC.
INCOME STATEMENT
FOR THE YEAR ENDED DECEMBER 31, 1989

Revenues		$492,000
Operating expenses (excluding depreciation)	$269,000	
Depreciation expense	21,000	290,000
Income from operations		202,000
Income tax expense		68,000
Net income		$134,000

Additional Information
(a) In 1989, the company paid an $18,000 cash dividend.
(b) The company obtained $150,000 cash through the issuance of long-term bonds.
(c) Land, building, and equipment were acquired for cash.

What does the reader have to know about these kinds of statements? Essentially, using the cash flow statement tells us how, starting with the net income we have derived in the income statement, this relates to the movement of cash into and out of the company. The subcategories that are considered important are the cash that is provided by operations, the cash that is provided (or utilized) for investment purposes (i.e., purchase of land, sale of equipment), as well as the financial activities of the firm (i.e., issuance of long-term debt, payments of cash dividends to shareholders, issuance of additional capital stock). This is a valuable statement and is now required to be disclosed by publicly owned companies in a regularly issued financial statement. It is not an optional statement any longer but one that companies are required to provide their readers under the financial accounting standards. It is a powerful tool in financial statement analysis because it pulls a company apart and enables a person to reflect on how management has decided to obtain and use the resources of the firm.

In analyzing a company using this statement one sees in the Wharton Company example the fact that significant amounts of cash are provided by operations and that significant amounts are being utilized for the expansion of the company via the purchase of additional equipment. It also shows that all of that expansion could not have been financed by cash provided by current operations. Rather, the company had to go to the outside and borrow additional money as well as dispose of land and equipment that already was on hand. This raises some questions:

Are the new investments appropriate in connection with the strategy of the company?

Was it appropriate to sell the land and equipment on hand?

Was too much money spent on new equipment and not enough paid in dividends to shareholders?

The statement also serves to give us cause to think about the fact that while $19,600 was reflected as net income, $36,600 of cash actually came into the company. Consequently, net income and cash inflow were not the same by a substantial margin.

Professional accountants spend a considerable amount of time on the subject of how information is accumulated and how statements of this type are constructed. It is not necessary that a person reading this book get into that amount of detail. What is important, however, is to highlight the major elements and some of the problems that crop up in order to understand these types of statements.

First of all, the statement brings home the fact that, in order to convert the net income per the income statement to cash provided by operations, it is important to realize that depreciation expense must be added back! Why is that? In essence it is because the spreading of the cost of an asset over its life has not resulted in reflecting a cash expense. The cash would have been laid out at the time the asset was acquired, but the depreciation expense over the years is not a cash flow item. Consequently, this adjustment is an important one.

Up to now we have concentrated on those items that flow through or affected changes in cash. However, the statement of changes in financial position must also include noncash transactions that are considered significant to the financing and investment activities of an enterprise. Thus the type of noncash transactions that are commonly reported in the statement of changes in financial positions are:

1. The issuance of short-term or long-term debt or equity securities to purchase temporary investments or noncurrent assets.
2. The conversion of debt or preferred stock into common stock.
3. The acquisition of temporary investments and long-term assets through gifts or donation or the forgiveness of a long-term obligation.
4. The retirement of debt through a sinking fund whereby assets are set aside for the ultimate retirement of the debt.
5. Reclassification of short-term to long-term debt or vice versa on the balance sheet.

These kinds of noncash transactions will not involve cash directly, but if they were not reflected in the statement, the reader would be given a misleading impression. An example of this is the situation illustrated below, whereby a company converted bonds having a book value of $50,000 for 50,000 shares of common stock with $1 par value. For a statement of changes of financial position, this information will be reported as follows:

Resources provided by issuance of common stock $50,000
Resources utilized to retire debt $50,000.

Showing these two transactions separately adds to the meaningfulness of the report.

Finally, extraordinary items that we discussed in Chapter 6 also are a factor in this statement of changes in financial position.

Whenever extraordinary gains or losses are involved, the statement generally starts with "Income before extraordinary items." To this amount are added back (or deducted) items recognized in determining income or loss but that did not use (or provide) cash. To illustrate, assume that Kenlon company reported net income of $39,000, which included an extraordinary gain of $9,000 (net of $3,000 tax) resulting from the sale of their only investment in equity securities (book value $16,000). Depreciation expense was $4,000 for the period in the statement of changes in financial position. The following information would be reported:

KENLON COMPANY
PARTIAL STATEMENT OF CHANGES IN FINANCIAL POSITION

Resources provided by operations:	
Income before extraordinary item	$30,000
Add (or deduct) items not affecting cash (Depreciation expense)	4,000
Cash provided by operations, exclusive of extraordinary item	34,000
Extraordinary item—sales of investment, including extraordinary gain of $9,000 (net of $3,000 tax)	25,000

One obvious question is worthy of note: What is the usefulness of the statement of changes in financial position?

First of all, the statement gives the readers the ability to assess the future cash flows in terms of the amount, timing, and the certainty of those cash flows.

Second, it provides a more reliable form than the income statement as to the quality of income because it involves a number of assumptions, estimates, and valuations. The funds flow data are considered more concrete and closer to cash than the income statement.

Third, operating capability is the ability of an enterprise to maintain a given physical level of operations. Whether an enterprise is able to maintain its operating capability, provide for future growth, and distribute dividends to the owners depends on whether adequate funds have been or will be generated. This type of statement assists in that evaluation.

Financial flexibility, as we indicated in Chapter 1, is the ability of an enterprise to take effective action to alter the amount and timing of cash flow in order to respond to unexpected needs and opportunities. The information on funds flow will be useful in determining whether a company will be able to survive such operating conditions.

Finally, the statement of changes in financial position provides answers to questions such as the following:

1. How was it possible to distribute dividends in excess of current earnings or in the presence of a net loss for the period?
2. How did cash (working capital) increase even though there was a net loss for the period?
3. How was the expansion in plant and equipment financed?
4. What happened to the proceeds from the sale of plant and equipment?
5. How was the retirement of debt accomplished?
6. What became of the assets derived from the increase in outstanding capital stock?
7. What became of the proceeds of the bond issue?
8. How was the increase in cash or working capital financed?

CHAPTER PERSPECTIVE

In this chapter we have explained the uses of the statement of changes in cash flow so that the business manager will be able to better manage the cash required to keep a business vibrant. With knowledge of this statement you will be able to determine how cash is generated from several sources—namely, the ongoing operations of the business, the selling of existing assets, the incurring of additional debt, as well as the issuing of new equity in the company. This chapter also gives you an appreciation of how to step back from an operation and get an overview of how the cash provided from the sources named above is being utilized in the expansion of the company, retirement of debt, and payment of dividends to shareholders. A knowledge of the statement of changes in cash flow coupled with the income statement discussed in Chapter 6 should provide a good background for obtaining know-how to analyze a company's operations.

How Do You Analyze The Financial Statements?

CHAPTER

8

INTRODUCTION AND MAIN POINTS

In this chapter we will begin to utilize the information gained in earlier chapters and analyze the financial statements we have been examining. The statements in and of themselves can be somewhat mysterious to business people even after they know how the statements are put together. In this chapter we are going to explain the different ways in which particular elements of a financial statement can be viewed in order to determine whether the company is doing well or poorly, either in relation to the company at an earlier period of time or in relation to competitors.

After studying the material in this chapter:

■ You will be able to analyze whether the company is in a satisfactory liquidity position by looking at ratios that relate to current assets and current liabilities of the company.

■ You will see how to evaluate the manner in which assets are flowing through the company by using activity ratios. These will enable you to determine how quickly the business is converting its assets into income.

■ You will be able to evaluate how profitable a company is through the use of profitability ratios. This will enable you to determine whether the activity in which the business is engaged is resulting in profits that are commensurate with that activity.

■ You will be able to evaluate the extent to which the liabilities of the company are being financed and the extent to which the assets of the company are providing sufficient coverage to pay off those liabilities.

■ You will know how to analyze the company not only from the standpoint of what it has done in a current year, but also from a comparative analysis standpoint by comparison with what it has done in prior years and also how it would compare with other businesses of similar size and activity.

The preceding discussion on the statement of changes in financial position is a good starting point for us to see how to look at and analyze financial statements. We have a feeling for how the resources of a business are recorded on the asset side of a balance sheet, and we have seen how liabilities to parties outside the company are reflected in that section on the balance sheet. We have also taken a look at how the ownership of a company is reflected in the capital stock and retained earnings sections of a balance sheet. Furthermore, we've taken a look at how the income statement records the revenue and expenses that go into the determination of the net income or loss from the recent activities of that company.

But just knowing where items are located on a financial statement is not being able to get full utilization of their value. This is where financial analysis comes in.

The type of financial analysis that takes place depends on the particular interest that the reader has in the enterprise. For example, short-term creditors (such as a bank) are primarily interested in the ability of the firm to pay its currently maturing obligations. The composition of the current assets and their relationship to short-term liabilities are examined closely to evaluate the short-run solvency of the company.

Bondholders, on the other hand, look more to long-term indicators such as the enterprise's capital structure, past and projected earnings, and changes in financial position in order to determine the ability to service the debt which they hold.

Stockholders present or prospective are also interested in many of the features considered by long-term creditors. Their examination is focused on the earnings picture because changes here greatly affect the market price of their investment.

The management of a company is, of necessity, concerned about the composition of its capital structure and about the changes and trends in earnings. This financial information has a direct influence on the type, amount, and cost of external financing that the company may obtain. In addition, the company finds financial information useful on a day-to-day operating basis in such areas as capital budgeting (by "capital budgeting" is meant the creation of an estimate of what funds will be needed for acquiring fixed assets and other major assets), break-even analysis ("break-even analysis" means the determination of what income will be needed to cover all the costs of the company's activities, so that, at the end of those activities, there will be a zero profit or loss), variance analysis and gross margin analysis ("gross margin analysis" means an evaluation of the extent to which the excess of sales over cost of sales is yielding a gross profit, which is suitable in the context of the type of business being conducted) for internal control purposes (by "internal control" is meant the system of checks and balances created within the company to make certain that all transactions entered into are reflected in the business records of the company and that they are recorded in amounts and at the times appropriate to accounting principles followed by the company).

Analysis of financial statements can be done by examining relationships between items on the income statement through ratios, and also by identifying trends by comparing the figures related to the same item over different periods of time. However, if all we do is compare ratios and do not know how to use such information, very little can be accomplished. A logical approach to financial statement analysis involves the following:

1. Knowing the questions for which we want an answer.
2. Knowing which ratios and comparisons are able to help us answer those questions.
3. Matching numbers 1 and 2 above to arrive at our conclusions.

CAUTIONARY NOTES

Before diving into such analysis, a few cautions have to be struck. First of all, we have to remember that much of the financial information we will be using is based on the past and not the future. Therefore, if we want to be able to predict things in the future, we have to realize that the numbers are working with have that deficiency.

Second, while some ratios may be very important to you and your thinking, avoid the tendency to hang your hat on just one ratio. For example, suppose you are interested in comparing what your return on investment in a company is, for comparison with the ability you have to put that money in a safer investment at a given rate of return. You might want to focus heavily on earnings per share, for instance. However, as we saw in Chapter 6, such numbers could give you a misleading result from your analysis.

Finally, as we saw in Chapter 5, there are limitations to the accounting numbers that would be used in any analysis. Controversy exists on accounting for installment sales, or long-term contracts, or depreciation policies for fixed assets, or inventory methods, or pensions cost, or leases. All can result in misleading conclusions if the analysis does not take these uncertainties into account.

With those cautions in mind, let us take a look at some of the ratios that assist in the analysis of financial statements.

LIQUIDITY RATIOS

This set of ratios tries to determine the short-term ability of an enterprise to pay its maturing obligations.

The first of these ratios is the *current ratio*, which consists of current assets divided by current liabilities, as illustrated below:

$$\text{Current ratio} = \frac{\text{Current assets}}{\text{Current liabilities}} = \frac{\$800,000}{\$575,000} = 1.39 \text{ times}$$

$$\text{Industry average} = 2.30 \text{ times}$$

The current ratio of 1.39:1, when compared to the industry average of 2.30:1, indicates that this company's safety factor to meet short-term obligations might be considered low. Consequently, it would raise a cautionary note to suppliers to the company as well as to internal management as to whether something can be done internally to improve the ratio.

An important point this first ratio indicates is that there is no magic number. Rather, some basis for comparison is needed. In this case the current ratio of the company is compared with an industry average. Without that industry comparison one could not conclude that the particular current ratio of the company is good or bad or average.

A second type of liquidity asset is called the *acid test* ratio, which is like the current ratio except that inventories are omitted. An example of this ratio is set out below:

$$\text{Acid Test Ratio} = \frac{\text{Cash} + \text{Marketable Securities} + \text{Net Receivables}}{\text{Current Liabilities}}$$

$$= \frac{\$490,000}{\$575,000} = .85 \text{ Times}$$

$$\text{Industry Average} = 1.20 \text{ Times}$$

The advantage to this ratio is that it overcomes the misinformation that could be taken from a current ratio if the company has a significant amount of its current assets tied up in slow-moving inventories. By removing inventories from the numerator, the acid test ratio can provide you with a better feel for the liquidity of the company.

Another type of liquidity ratio is the *defensive interval* ratio. This is computed by dividing so-called defensive assets (cash, marketable securities, and net receivables) by projected daily expenditures from operations. The ratio measures the time span a firm can operate on present liquid assets without resorting to revenue from future resources. The projected daily expenditures can be computed by dividing the cost of goods sold plus selling and administrative expenses plus other ordinary cash expenses by 365 days. We can see below an example of how this computation would be made.

$$\text{Defensive-interval measure} = \frac{\text{Defensive assets}}{\substack{\text{Projected daily operational} \\ \text{expenditures (based on past} \\ \text{expenditures) minus noncash} \\ \text{charges}}}$$

$$= \$490,000 \div \frac{\$1,525,000 - \$150,000}{365}$$

$$= 130 \text{ days}$$

Industry average $= 80$ days

This illustration indicates that the company in question would have 130 days' worth of liquid assets that it could use to cover its operating expenses requiring cash outlays. The industry average in general would be 80 days. Consequently, one could conclude that this company is in reasonably good shape from that standpoint.

From these liquidity ratios we can see that no one ratio gives a complete picture. But, depending on your familiarity with the company and which type of ratios might be more important, you could use all of them, yet put more stress on one versus another.

ACTIVITY RATIOS

Another way of evaluating the company is to determine how quickly assets can be turned into cash (i.e. how liquid are the accounts receivable and inventory?) This type of information can provide data on how efficiently the enterprise is using its assets and becomes, in part, a measurement of the performance of management of the company.

Once such ratio in this regard is *receivable turnover*, which is computed by the dividing net sales by the average accounts receivable outstanding during the year. An example of this is set out below:

$$\text{Accounts receivable turnover}$$
$$equals$$
$$\frac{\text{Net sales}}{\text{average trade receivables (net)}}$$
$$equals$$
$$\$1,600,000 \div \frac{\$350,000 + \$300,000}{2}$$
$$equals$$

4.92 or every 74 days (365 days ÷ 4.92)
Industry Average = 7.15 or every 51 days

This information provides an indication of how successful a firm is in collecting its outstanding receivables. The faster this turnover takes place, the quicker the company is making sales and converting receivables into cash. The term "lockup" is used in this analysis to indicate the amount of time that the company's money is locked up in accounts receivable and not collected. This indicates the period of time over which the company is acting as a bank in providing capital to its customers. This particular example would indicate that the industry average has companies locking up their cash for 51 days, whereas the company has locked up its cash for 74 days. Should the company start charging customers interest for the use of this cash? This is the type of issue that an analysis of this ratio would raise.

Another ratio involves *inventory turnover*, which is computed by dividing the average inventory into the cost of goods sold. This ratio measures how quickly the inventory has been sold and also indicates over how many days inventory is locked up before being sold. This kind of analysis would give the person doing the analysis some idea of how much of a company's own money is invested in inventory, carrying this on the books of the company before the products are actually sold. An example of this is set forth in the following:

$$\text{Inventory turnover} = \frac{\text{Cost of goods sold}}{\text{Average inventory}} = \frac{\$1,000,000}{\$310,000 + \$250,000}$$

$$= 3.57 \text{ times or every } 102 \text{ days } (365 \text{ days} \div 3.57)$$

Industry average $= 4.62$ or every 79 days

Generally speaking, the higher the inventory turnover, the better the enterprise is performing. However, it is also possible that the enterprise is not carrying enough inventory to serve its customers because it wants to have too small an investment in inventory. This provides the reader with a trade-off consideration as to what amount of ratio for that company is indicative of efficient investment versus how much is indicative of poor customer service. In this particular example, the fact that the industry average is 79 days of inventory whereas the company has 102 days would indicate that perhaps the company is not doing a good job. On the other hand, it might be that the company is bending over backwards to make sure that it does not go out of stock, or stock out, on a frequent basis, and thus provides excellent customer service.

A further activity ratio would be one of *asset turnover*, which is determined by dividing the average total assets of the company into net sales for the period. This is illustrated in the following example:

$$\text{Asset turnover} = \frac{\text{Net Sales}}{\text{Average total assets}} = \frac{\$1,600,000}{\dfrac{\$2,250,000 + \$2,100,000}{2}} = .74$$

Industry average $= .94$

This ratio indicates how efficiently the company is utilizing its assets to generate sales. If the turnover ratio is low, the company has to either use its assets more efficiently or dispose of some of them. The problem with this turnover calculation is that it places a premium on using older assets because their book value is low. Remember that our discussion of the balance sheet indicated that historical cost is the traditional method of recording assets of this type. As a result, we are measuring historical cost on the asset side with current dollars on the sale side. For this reason, this particular ratio should be used only in combination with others in evaluating the efficiency of the company.

PROFITABILITY RATIOS

In addition to liquidity and activity ratios a series of ratios exists that determines how profitable a company will be or has been. These ratios answer such questions as: Was the net income adequate? What rate of return does it represent? What is the rate of income by various activities? What amount was paid in dividends to the shareholders? What amount was earned by different people owning different types of equity in the company?

One such ratio is *profit margin on sales*, which is computed by dividing net income by net sales for the period. This ratio indicates that the company is achieving either above-average or below-average rates of profit on each sales dollar received. It is illustrated by the following example:

$$\text{Profit margin on sales} = \frac{\text{Net income}}{\text{Net sales}} = \frac{\$150,000}{\$1,600,000} = 9.4\%$$

$$\text{Industry average} = 6\%$$

Compared with the industry average of 6 percent, this company is earning a 9.4 percent return on its sales. When used in conjunction with the asset turnover ratio, this ratio can determine the rate of return on total assets, as illustrated below.

$$\text{Rate of return on assets} = \text{Profit margin on sales} \times \text{Asset turnover}$$

$$\text{Rate of return on assets} = \frac{\text{Net income}}{\text{Net sales}} \times \frac{\text{Net sales}}{\text{Average total assets}}$$

$$\frac{\$150,000}{\$1,600,000} \times \frac{\$1,600,000}{\dfrac{\$2,250,000 + \$2,100,000}{2}}$$

$$= 6.9\%$$

$$\text{Industry average} = 5.6\%$$

In essence, this ratio tries to determine how the company is utilizing the assets of the enterprise to produce net income. Once again the illustration indicates that the company is doing better than the industry average. This is also important in measuring performance of management, since management is a group of people that has control of these assets and determines how they are to be deployed to generate income. It should be noted that the profit margin on sales does not answer the question of how profitable an enterprise was for a given period of time. Only by determining how many times the assets turned over during a period of time is it possible to determine the amount of net income earned on total assets.

For example, grocery stores and discount stores have a small profit margin on sales with a high turnover of assets. Other retail enterprises, on the other hand, such as jewelry and furniture stores, generate a relatively high profit margin on sales but have a smaller inventory turnover. It is therefore important that the reader know the type of business a firm is in and what can be expected of both these aspects of turnover and profitability.

Another ratio helpful for analysis is the *rate of return on common stock equity*. This ratio is determined from net income after interest, taxes, and preferred dividends divided by average common stockholder equity. It is illustrated by the following example:

$$\text{Rate of return on common stock equity} = \frac{\text{Net income minus preferred dividends}}{\text{Average common stockholders' equity}}$$

$$= \frac{\$150,000 - \$950,000 + \$1,100,000}{2}$$

$$= 14.6\%$$

Industry average $= 9.5\%$

When the rate of return on total assets is lower than the rate of return on common stockholder investment, the enterprise is said to be trading on the equity ("trading on the equity" is the practice of borrowing money in a business which, when added to the investment by the stockholders, will enable the company to acquire a larger amount of assets; the concept is that, where the investment by stockholders itself will not be sufficient to conduct the business at the size that is desirable, the borrowing of money provides leverage to the equity in the company). The game of trading on the equity increases the company's financial risk but enhances residual earnings, when the rate of return on assets exceeds the cost of debt capital. Thus, if you are conducting a business and can get other people's capital working for you, you have the opportunity of increasing the value of your personal investment. This is also known as "leveraging," or borrowing money from outside parties at a cost that is less than what you earn on the assets acquired from the borrowing. The difference then goes into your pocket as the equity owner of the company.

We have already discussed to some extent in Chapter 6 earnings per share, which is considered a profitability ratio. Often earnings per share can be increased simply by reducing the number of shares outstanding through the repurchase of the company's own stock. This is known as treasury stock. It must also be realized that the earnings per share figure fails to recognize the probable increase in the base of the stockholders' investment. That is, earnings per share will probably increase year after year if the corporation reinvests earnings in the business, because a larger earning figure is generated without a corresponding increase in the number of shares outstanding. Because the public attaches such importance to earnings per share these days, caution must be exercised in using this ratio.

We have also available for analysis the price/earnings ratio, which is the market price of a share of stock divided by the annual earnings per share. The financial press sometimes uses the price/earnings ratio as a magic number. But there is danger in the use of this statistic. There are many reasons why the price/earnings ratio of a company is high or low. Important factors include relative risk, stability of earnings, trends in earnings, and the market's perception of the growth potential of the stock. Indeed, given the sophistication with which securities analysts are able to factor the potential for the future into a company's activities, it is often said that the price/earnings ratios are a good indication of what could be expected of a company in the future. To put it in another way, the P/E ratio is based not so much on past earnings but future expected earnings of a company. In some cases a company's P/E may go down, even when it has had a good year if the results do not come up to the analysts' predictions. If analysts believe that a good year should have been even better, the P/E may go down.

A final profitability ratio is called the *payout ratio*, which is the ratio consisting of cash dividends divided by net income. It is important to some investors that a fairly substantial payout ratio exists, although speculators view appreciation in the value of stock as more important than dividend payout. An example of the payout ratio is set out below:

$$\text{Payout ratio} = \frac{\text{Cash dividends}}{\text{Net income less preferred dividends}} = \frac{\$67,500}{\$150,000 - 50,000} = 67.5\%$$

A closely related ratio is dividend yield. That is simply cash dividends per share divided by the market share of the stock. This ratio gives the investor some idea of the rate of return that will be received in cash dividends in the short run from their investment.

COVERAGE RATIOS

The coverage ratios help in predicting the long-run solvency of the firm. They are of interest primarily to bondholders, who need some indication of the measure of protection available to them. In addition, these trends indicate part of the risk involved in investing in common stock, because the more debt that is added to the capital structure, the more uncertain is the return on the common stock.

The first such ratio is *debt to total assets*, which provides creditors with some idea of the corporation's ability to withstand losses without impairing the interests of creditors. The lower this ratio is, the more buffer there is available to creditors before the corporation becomes insolvent. It is computed by dividing the total debt of the company by the total assets, as reflected in the following:

$$\text{Debt to total assets} = \frac{\text{Debt}}{\substack{\text{Total assets} \\ \text{or equities}}} = \frac{\$1,300,000}{\$2,250,000} = 58\%$$

$$\text{Industry average} = 38\%$$

From this it can be seen that the industry average is much lower than that of the company being analyzed. Consequently, it indicates a danger point with regard to whether the company has overleveraged itself by incurring too much debt.

Another coverage ratio is *times interest earned*, which is computed by dividing income before interest charges and taxes by the interest charge. It stresses the importance of a company covering all of the interest charges, as illustrated by the following:

$$\substack{\text{Times interest} \\ \text{earned}} = \frac{\substack{\text{Income before taxes} \\ \text{and interest charges}}}{\text{interest charges}} = \frac{\$300,000}{\$50,000} = 6 \text{ times}$$

$$\text{Industry average} = 4 \text{ times}$$

The company in this example would seem to have a significant amount of income to cover the interest charges, and consequently might be able to leverage itself even more.

Another coverage ratio, *book value per share*, is used for evaluating a company's net worth and the changes in it from year to year. Book value per share of stock is the amount each stockholder would receive if the company were liquidated on the basis of the amount reported on the balance sheet. This figure loses much of its relevance if the valuations on the balance sheet do not approximate the fair market value of the assets. As we have seen in Chapter 1, the use of historical figures as a basis for book value determination makes this a less valuable ratio. However, it is a good basis for a way of comparing with market value per share to see to what extent the company might be undervalued. This certainly is a technique used by many takeover artists in determining whether they might be able to buy a company with its own assets. This is done by acquiring the target company and financing the buyout by selling some of the assets of the company at their higher fair-market values. An example of this will be found below:

$$\text{Book value per share} \; = \; \frac{\text{Common stockholders' equity}}{\text{Outstanding shares}} \; = \; \frac{\$900,000}{30,000} \; = \; \$30.00$$

If the fair market value per share were $50, this company might be a takeover target.

Finally, coverage can be computed with the *cash flow per share*, a calculation that consists of net income plus noncash adjustments divided by outstanding shares. This amount represents either the flow of cash through the enterprise or the residual of the cash received minus the cash dispersed divided by the outstanding shares of stock. It is frequently used to approximate the amount of cash generated internally. It should be noted that the accounting profession strongly recommends that isolated statistics of working capital or cash provided from operations *not* be presented in the annual report to shareholders.[1]

Having gone through these various ratios on liquidity, activity, profitability and coverage several cautionary notes should be pointed out at this point.

First, it should be noted that there are limitations on ratios because they are based on historical costs. This can lead to distortion in measuring performance. Second, investors must remember that where estimated items (such as depreciation and amortization) are significant, income ratios lose some of their credibility. Third, it is a difficult problem to achieve comparability among firms in a given industry, because of the latitude in accounting standards that may be used in accounting for fairly major items. In order to do this on a more precise basis you would have to have sufficient information about other companies with regard to how they treat such major items as inventory methods, bad debt for accounts receivable, depreciation of fixed assets, and the recording of discount and premium on debt obligations.

COMPARATIVE ANALYSIS

The ratio analyses discussed earlier provided a single item for one given point or period of time. A comparative analysis enables an analyst to concentrate on a given item and to determine whether it appears to be growing or diminishing year by year and the proportion of such change. A relative comparative analysis of items within the company is generally facilitated by the fact that many annual reports give figures for a period of five or ten years, so that key items can be compared over time.

Accounting Research Bulletin #43 concluded that presentation of comparative financial statements in annual and other reports enhances the usefulness of such reports and brings out more clearly the nature and trends of current changes affecting the enterprise. An illustration of a five-year condensed statement with additional reporting data is presented in Table 8-1. From this report one can see how sales have been changing over the years and what trends of growth or decline might be taking place in one or several of these items.

This comparative treatment is an important technique to keep in mind. Even where companies do not regularly present such information, you should request that a company being analyzed provide information of this type over a number of years so that year-by-year analysis can be made more effectively.

A further technique is called *common sized analysis*. This uses percentages to help evaluate an enterprise and consists of reducing a series of related amounts to a series of percentages of a given base. For example, items in an income statement are frequently exressed as a percentage of sales or sometimes as a percentage of cost of goods sold. A balance sheet may be analyzed from the basis of percentage to total assets. This reduction of absolute dollar amounts to percentages facilitates comparison between companies of different sizes. This is illustrated by the report of the Monger Chemical Company on page 000.

TABLE 8-1
Year-to-Year Comparisons

(Dollars in millions except per-share figures)	1986	1985	1984	1983	1982
Earnings data on sales to customers:					
Domestic	$3,972.0	$3,989.9	$3,735.9	$3,610.5	$3,304.0
International	3,030.9	2,431.4	2,388.6	2,362.4	2,456.9
Total sales	7,002.9	6,421.3	6,124.5	5,972.9	5,760.9
Interest income	99.9	107.3	84.5	82.9	88.9
Royalties and miscellaneous	65.0	48.1	38.0	49.4	49.3
Total revenues	7,167.8	6,576.7	6,247.0	6,105.2	5,899.1
Cost of products sold	2,630.1	2,594.2	2,469.4	2,471.8	2,450.9
Selling, distribution and administrative expenses	2,867.9	2,516.0	2,488.4	2,352.9	2,248.8
Research expense	521.3	471.1	421.2	407.8	363.2
Interest expense	87.4	74.8	86.1	88.3	74.4
Interest expense capitalized	(21.8)	(28.9)	(35.0)	(39.6)	(46.3)
Redirection charges	540.0	—	—	—	—
Other expenses	152.1	50.3	61.8	99.9	20.9
Total costs and expenses	6,777.0	5,677.5	5,491.9	5,381.1	5,111.9
Earnings before provision for taxes on income	390.8	899.2	755.1	724.1	787.2
Provision for taxes on income	61.3	285.5	240.6	235.1	263.8
Earnings before extraordinary charge	329.5	613.7	514.5	489.0	523.4
Extraordinary charge (net of taxes)	—	—	—	—	(50.0)
Net earnings	$ 329.5	$ 613.7	$ 514.5	$ 489.0	$ 473.4

MONGER CHEMICAL

	1987	1986	Difference	% Change Inc. (dec.)
Cost of sales	$1,000.0	$850.0	$150.0	17.6
Depreciation and amortization	150.0	150.0	0	0
Selling and administrative expense	225.0	150.0	75.0	50.0
Interest expense	50.0	25.0	25.0	100.0
Taxes	100.0	75.0	25.0	33.3

This example gives horizontal analysis since it indicates proportionate change of an item over a period of time. A vertical analysis is set forth below:

MONGER CHEMICAL
INCOME STATEMENT
(000,000 OMITTED)

	Amount	Percentage of Total Revenue
Net sales	$1,600.0	96%
Other revenue	75.0	4
Total revenue	1,675.0	100
Less		
Cost of goods sold	$1,000.0	60
Depreciation and amortization	150.0	9
Selling and administrative expenses	225.0	13
Interest expense	50.0	3
Income tax	100.0	6
Total expenses	$1,525.0	91
Net income	$ 150.0	9

This type of analysis helps an individual to see the piece of the pie that becomes cost of goods sold, depreciation, selling and administrative expenses, interest expense, and income tax expense.

From this chapter, then, we can see that the analysis of financial statements is an art as well as a science. However, you need not be an expert to get the feeling for general trends and composition of what is going on at a company. Many people stare at financial statements as if there was some kind of mystery involved in them. As in the case of the medical profession, the result of tests that are taken on our body give a doctor an opportunity of watching trends and also making a diagnosis based on those trends.

Analysis of financial statements is quite similar. It is hoped that with an understanding of what goes into financial statements and the use of these ratios and comparative tools, you would be in a position to have at least some comfortable feeling as to what is going on in the company of which you are a customer, or a supplier, or lender of funds, or any person outside the company. As we look into managerial accounting in more detail in a later chapter, it will give us a feeling for how these techniques are used by people inside the company.

CHAPTER PERSPECTIVE

In this chapter we have given you an important set of tools for utilizing the accounting information discussed in earlier chapters. You no longer are only aware of what financial statements contain, but rather you are also in the position to pull apart individual accounts in the financial statements to determine to what extent they are pointing you in the direction of success or failure. This chapter does not contain all of the analytical tools that can be utilized in analyzing financial statements. However, the material presented should whet your interest in terms of what fundamental analytical tools are available and lead you as a business person to other types of analysis ratios that can help you determine whether the company is moving in the right direction. This type of analysis is important not only in keeping track of what is going on in the company now, but also in giving you some feeling for how divisions in the same company might compare to each other or how the entire company stacks up against other companies with which you are familiar in the industry. The analytical tools discussed in this chapter can be of interest to people outside the company. It now remains to move forward to accounting information that will be more useful operating the company internally.

FOOTNOTES

1 *"Reporting Changes in Financial Position" APB Opinion #17 (New York: AICPA, 1979), paragraph 15.*

Managerial Accounting: Using Accounting For Internal Purposes

INTRODUCTION AND MAIN POINTS

In this chapter we are going to expand your knowledge of the use of accounting for internal purposes in the company. In the earlier discussions of accounting, we were looking at information of interest to people outside the company, i.e., suppliers of inventory, lenders of money to the company, shareholders of the company, the Internal Revenue Service, and all the other entities that have some stake in knowing a company's financial position. In this chapter we will begin delving into accounting as a tool to help a company set goals for the future and to monitor this activity so that it moves along in a manner consistent with those goals. In this regard, managerial accounting is more future-oriented than the financial accounting concepts we have discussed so far.

After studying the material in this chapter:

■ You will have a basic understanding of what managerial accounting involves from an overall standpoint.

■ You will know the basic concepts of managerial accounting from the standpoint of planning for the future and controlling activities so that they are consistent with the planning.

■ You will see the difference between managerial accounting and financial accounting reports.

■ You will have an idea of the professional standards that must be met by people concentrating on managerial accounting as opposed to financial accounting.

Managerial accounting is designed to provide a comprehensive and contemporary foundation for the kinds of accounting data used by managers in organizations today. As indicated in Chapter 1, it is differentiated from financial accounting in that financial accounting applies to recording accounting information for use by people outside the company, whereas managerial accounting is used by people inside the company. The focus of managerial accounting is on the acquisition, analysis, and application of accounting information in the management decision process of a business.

Managerial accounting also interrelates with tax accounting in that taxation very often requires information with regard to determining the collectibility of accounts receivable, the determination of costs of inventory and their relationship to fair market values, the very important area of budgeting capital expenditures (such as plant and equipment), the determination of how research costs are to be taken into account, and the methods of financing the company through the incurring of debt as well as the issuance of equity securities.

Managerial accounting is divided into a number of areas, which we will consider separately. However, at this point it is important that the reader have a good overview of what the elements of managerial accounting encompass.

MANAGERIAL ACCOUNTING STEPS

First we must have a clear understanding of the various elements in managerial accounting—the basic raw material that is essential to the utilization of the data. This involves the understanding of the classification of the various costs of doing business—the expenses that are incurred by a business and the values placed on those expenses in order to ascertain whether the business is operating on a profitable basis)—as well as how such costs flow through the operations of the company. It also involves a knowledge of what we will soon see are called variable costs (a "variable cost" is a cost that differs with the level of activity that is conducted by a business) and fixed costs (a "fixed cost" is an expense that remains the same during the accounting period regardless of the level of business activity that is entered into) and how they are used in the managerial accounting area.

Second, we must have a basic understanding of the fundamental costs in a managerial accounting system. In the vernacular, these are often described as "job order" costing and "process costing" systems. The first involves the accumulation of costs that relate to the operation of a particular project or job (i.e., a cost associated with the building of a machine). The second involves costs associated with an entire process (i.e., the flow of costs that have been incurred in the process of manufacturing automobiles).

Third, for our managerial cost foundation, it is important to know how managers in companies successfully use accounting information in planning future decisions. This requires that one have an understanding of how costs relate to volume of production and how these two in turn relate to the profitability (or loss) of an activity. In developing plans for reaching target objectives at this stage, we will have to understand a bit more of the budgeting process that ensures that resources are available to reach the targets. It is also at this point that we will be identifying and analyzing costs relevant to decision-making where the project is not recurring.

Fourth, we will look into the subject of how to prepare and analyze reports that managers use in controlling the organization once the planning process is put in place. This involves a knowledge of what is called responsibility accounting and covers the control of direct material and direct labor costs through the use of standard costs in the accounting system ("standard cost" is a cost that is attributable to a particular activity on the assumption that the activity is conducted in a manner consistent with efficient operation; that is, a company will determine certain norms as to how its activity should be conducted and relate certain costs to the business assuming it is conducted at that efficient level). We will also discuss the utilization of flexible budgets to control overhead costs ("flexible budgets" are estimates of cost in the future that are changed or adjusted as the activity of the business changes). This is important for managers that are involved in reporting on expense, revenue, and profit centers as well as investment centers (a "profit center" is a portion of a business that is measured on the basis of its excess of revenues over expenses; a profit center is expected to earn a profit and is measured on that standard).

Finally, we look at capital expenditure ("capital expenditure" is an outlay of funds for those assets that are long term in nature and will last longer than one accounting period), including the impact of the tax law on such expenditures as well as the cost allocation in arriving at the evaluation of the efficiency of the capital expenditures. This discussion will be tied into our earlier analysis of financial statements, including the statement of cash flow.

With this overall background, let us look at the basic concepts of managerial accounting.

BASIC CONCEPTS

Managerial accounting assists business people in planning and controlling decisions. (We have to recall that planning involves establishing objectives and goals as well as structures for accomplishing them.) Most planning decisions require managerial accounting information, including:

1. What price should we charge for a product?
2. How many units of a product should we manufacture?
3. Should we expand production facilities?
4. How much money should we spend on research and advertising?
5. Should we rely solely on cash receipts from operations to cover capital expenditures?

Answers to these questions require estimates of future revenue and costs. Managerial decisions concern financial effects in the future. They must be based on historical information of the type we find in financial accounting reports, which are of course based on financial performance.

Control decisions involve adjusting the activities needed to implement a business plan to achieve desired results. Control decisions are made only when actual results differ significantly from expected results. For that reason, the first step in making control decisions is to compare actual and expected results.

Some typical control decisions requiring managerial accounting information include:

1. What action to take to bring actual sales in line with expected sales.
2. Whether to authorize overtime to make up for lost production value.
3. Whether to increase advertising to improve sales.

All of these decisions impact future revenues and costs.

Whereas financial accounting reports tend to cover a company's activities as a whole, managerial accounting reports tend to cover specific product lines, divisions, sales territory, and customer groups by dollar volume or number of orders. This is because those types of operating decisions are made at the division or territory level.

Also unlike financial accounting reports, managerial accounting reports are not subject to externally imposed reporting standards. For that reason they may include subjective information. For example, in setting monthly sales targets, management is generally more interested in the sales manager's subjective estimates of future sales than in the objective value of past sales. This is not to imply that last month's sales are not important; often, they are the best indicator of next month's sales. However, forecast sales figures are more important than past statistics when setting targets.

Managers may actually make bad choices if they use financial accounting data to make decisions. For example, marketing and production managers want to be informed of sales orders as they are received; that is, before products are shipped. Such information helps the production manager to decide which products to produce and in what quantities. But financial accounting reports only contain the revenue and costs of past orders shipped. Production must be scheduled based on orders to be shipped this month and the next month.

The significant differences between financial and management accounting are summarized in Table 9–1.

TABLE 9–1
SUMMARY OF DIFFERENCE BETWEEN
FINANCIAL AND MANAGERIAL ACCOUNTING

Financial Accounting	*Managerial Accounting*
1. Information is meant primarily for external users.	Information is meant primarily for internal users.
2. Information summarizes the financial effects of past events.	Information forecasts the financial effects of future events.
3. Decisions on what to report are guided by generally accepted account principles.	Decisions on what to report are guided by the information's relevance to a manager's needs.
4. Data are based on objective observations.	Data are based partially on subjective judgments.
5. Reports cover whole organizations and provide few details.	Reports cover product lines, divisions, and sales territories in detail.
6. Reports are designed for general use.	Reports are designed for special purposes.

Managerial accounting involves the question of whether there is a professional accreditation in the area of managerial accounting as there is in financial accounting. The answer is yes. You may recall that, in the discussion of financial accounting, we indicated that the professional can attain the position of Certified Public Accountant (CPA) by taking a professional examination. That accreditation enables the individual to perform an independent audit of financial statements and provide an opinion on those statements as to whether they fairly present the financial position of the company. In addition, managerial accountants may achieve the status of Certified Management Account (CMA) from the Institute of Certified Management Accountants (ICMA). This CMA program requires candidates to pass a series of examinations that meet educational and professional standards to qualify for and maintain the certificate.

The CMA exam has five parts that cover the following topics:
1. Economic and business finance.
2. Organization and behavior, including ethical considerations.
3. Public reporting standards, auditing, and taxation.
4. Periodic reporting for internal and external purposes.
5. Decision analysis, including modeling and information systems.

The ICMA, by including basic management topics on the CMA exam, has emphasized the dual role of the managerial accountant—namely, business person and accountant.

CHAPTER PERSPECTIVE

In this chapter we have begun to give you exposure to the accounting method that is used to run a business from an internal standpoint. We delve into more detail in the following chapters. At this point however, you should have an appreciation for the fact that there is quite a difference in the ways the costs of a company are viewed, with the methods discussed in earlier chapters dealing with financial statement accounting representing one approach and the methods that will be coming up dealing with managerial accounting representing another approach. We have introduced you to such terms as fixed costs, variable costs, and standard costs, all of which are new to the discussion in this book up to this point. As a start to gaining more knowledge about managerial accounting, we will now look at the way in which costs are classified for purposes of assisting owners and managers to run their businesses in a more efficient manner.

The Need for Cost Classification and Cost Flow Through the Business

CHAPTER
10

INTRODUCTION AND MAIN POINTS

In this chapter we are going to expand your knowledge of the way in which costs can be classified in order to put you in the position of running your business in a better way. We will look at costs from the point of view of a person actually running a manufacturing or service business, so that he or she will see how to set goals for the profitability of the company and to monitor those goals on a going-forward basis.

After studying the material in this chapter:

■ You will see the difference between costs that go into determining the expense of creating a product versus those costs that relate to a period of time in which the business is being conducted.

■ You will have an appreciation for the way in which costs are determined in a service company so that people conducting the business will be able to have a preliminary understanding of how to properly match costs with revenues.

■ You will understand the classification of costs in manufacturing operations, which are more complicated than service organizations.

■ You will see how costs flow through a company from the earlier stages of raw materials purchased through the stage of inventory that is not yet complete and ready for sale, to finished products that are available for sale to the customer. The flow of costs through a company is important in the determination of what the potential for profit or loss of the company might be.

■ You will have a preliminary understanding of the costing system involved when a company makes more than one product. In these situations an analysis is required to determine what costs relate to which products, in order to determine which products should be continued and which should be discontinued, in order for the company to be more profitable.

Accounting costs are classified in numerous ways. To prepare financial statements, accountants must associate costs with specific time periods (see Chapter 6). The classification of costs into product and period costs allows accountants to do that. The most complex cost-classification systems are found in manufacturing organizations, where special statements must be prepared to determine the cost of goods sold. At this point we will concentrate on only the most basic cost classification, that which is needed to perform the analysis of what costs relate to a particular period of time. This will provide the foundation for you to be able to use accounting for business management.

PRODUCT COST VS. PERIOD COST

In both financial and managerial accounting, costs have to be related to time periods. In financial accounting, income statements and balance sheets are prepared quarterly and annually for shareholders. In managerial accounting, reports comparing actual results to expected (budget) results are prepared monthly, quarterly, and annually. Most planning and control decisions in a company are also related to time periods. Actual results are compared with budgeted results at the end of each month to measure performance.

Costs related to time periods are called either product costs or period costs. *Period costs* are selling or administrative costs that usually cannot be associated with particular products or sales. For example, the president's salary is an administrative cost not directly associated with particular products. General liability insurance is another such cost. Accountants match those expenses against revenue for the business periods in which they were incurred. This is the reason why they are called period costs.

Any period cost assigned to an unconsumed item or unexpired contract is classified as an asset rather than an expense. This cost is referred to as a prepaid expense. For example, assume that on January 1989 a company purchased a three-year insurance policy for $9,000. At the end of the year, one year of the three-year policy has expired. Therefore, $3,000, which is the cost of insurance for 1989, must be deducted from the year's revenue in order to properly match cost and revenue. The remaining cost of $6,000 is treated as a prepaid expense and will be deducted from revenue as the insurance expires.

A product cost, on the other hand, is a cost incurred to acquire or manufacture inventory for sale. A department store purchases finished inventory items from a supplier, while an automobile producer manufactures its finished inventory. Therefore, for the store and other merchandising companies, product cost is the purchase price of goods acquired for resale. A manufacturing company, on the other hand, has a great many product costs, including the cost of raw materials purchased plus the sum of all costs incurred to convert those materials into finished products. Included in the latter sum would be the cost of the labor, machinery, equipment, and buildings used to produce the finished product.

Like period costs, product costs are used by both financial and managerial accountants. Financial accountants use product costs to determine the cost of inventories and cost of goods sold. Managerial accountants use product costs to evaluate the profitability of the products a firm sells.

Like the unexpired period costs illustrated above, product costs are treated as assets until the products are sold. Product costs that are assigned to units of inventory are referred to as inventoriable costs. When products are shipped to customers, these costs become expenses and are deducted from sales revenue. In this way the expenses and revenues are reported in the same period as the revenues are earned.

For example, assume that on January 1, 1989, Muir Computer Company acquired 100 computers at a wholesale cost of $2,000 each. The company plans to sell these machines for $4,000 each. However, during the year only 10 computers were sold. Product costs of $20,000 for these computers sold will be subtracted from the $40,000 in revenue from the sales. The $180,000 product costs for the remaining 90 computers are deferred until the machines are sold. This process of associating product costs with the sales of a product (and period costs with the time period in which the cost expired) is called matching costs with revenues, and is essential to using accounting to better manage a business.

To better illustrate this point, look at Figure 10-1 to determine how total costs are divided along the lines just described.

COST CLASSIFICATION IN A SERVICE COMPANY

The foregoing description has dealt primarily with the purchase and sale of tangible items, on the one hand, and the manufacturing and sale of tangible items on the other hand. Service companies such as consulting firms, auto repair shops, health

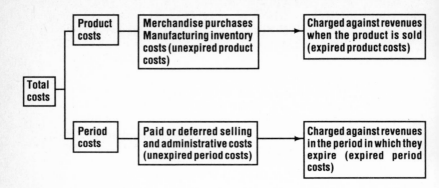

FIG. 10-1 *Dividing total costs*

maintenance organizations, banks and brokerage houses, produce services rather than products. Services are generally delivered as they are produced. Therefore, in service industries there is no product inventory as such, and costs relate to the time period in which they expired. The distinction between product and period cost is thus not particularly useful to most service companies. What is useful for service companies is to divide their costs into "direct" and "indirect" classes.

Direct costs are those costs that are specifically traceable to a specific service, such as salaries paid to accountants and mechanics. These costs are similar to the product cost of a merchandising or manufacturing company. They are costs of providing salable "products" (in this case, a service) to a customer. The direct costs for performing specific services are matched with the revenue they generate.

Indirect costs are those that cannot be traced to a particular service, such as insurance or office rent. Like period costs in a merchandising or manufacturing company, indirect costs are generally deducted from revenue in the period in which the cost expires.

At the end of an accounting period, some services are usually incomplete. The expected revenue associated with these services must be estimated because they are really an asset that should appear on the balance sheet. For example, a service company might estimate the amount of such revenue by multiplying the ratio of incurred direct cost to total expected direct cost times the total expected revenue when the service is completed.

To illustrate this point look at the income statement and current assets of the Maricela Consulting Company. The first expense listed is employee compensation and fringe benefits. It is a direct expense of earning the revenue of this company. All other expenses are indirect expenses. Notice that the balance sheet contains no entry for inventory as it would in a merchandising or manufacturing company. Instead, there is an account for services performed on December 31 but not yet billed to clients. This amount was estimated on the basis of direct service costs incurred to the date of the balance sheet.

MARICELA CONSULTING COMPANY
INCOME STATEMENT
FOR THE YEAR ENDED DECEMBER 31, 1988

Fees for professional service		$500,000
Employee compensation and fringe benefits*	$245,000	
Rent of office facilities	30,000	
Training and research	20,000	
Personnel insurance and litigation	6,000	
Other expenses	25,000	
Total expenses		336,000
Operating income		$164,000

MARICELA CONSULTING COMPANY
CURRENT ASSET SECTION OF THE BALANCE SHEET
DECEMBER 31, 1988

Current Assets	
Cash	$ 25,000
Accounts receivable	63,000
Unbilled services, at estimated** Billable rate	50,000
Prepaid expenses	14,000
Total current assets	$152,000

* *The asterisked costs represent direct costs in the income statement.*

** *The unbilled services, at estimated billable rates, are based on the direct costs of services unfurnished at year end.*

To summarize, service companies have no need to classify costs as product or period costs. Instead they divide costs into direct and indirect. They match the direct costs of providing their services against the revenue they earn for their services. They subtract their indirect costs from revenue in the period in which they expire.

COST CLASSIFICATION IN A MANUFACTURING COMPANY

Like a merchandising company a manufacturing company divides its expenses into product and period costs. Computing period costs is done similarly in both types of companies. However, because manufacturing companies make their own products rather than buy the products they sell, their product costs are much more complicated than those of a merchandising company. For example, a steel company converts material such as iron ore into finished products such as sheet metal. The company's product costs include not only the cost of purchasing the iron but also the cost of converting the raw material into saleable products. Product costs include the cost of the raw materials, the cost of the steelworkers used in processing those materials, and the cost of occupying and operating the steel mills in which the sheet metal is made. These product costs are counted as assets until a product is sold and the revenue from the sale is recorded in the income statement.

Examine the income statement for the Diane Manufacturing Company. On the surface this information is similar to that of the Hamm Computer Company demonstrated earlier. The difference is in the section of the product costs. Unlike a merchandising company, which refers to the value of the goods ready for sale as merchandise inventory, a manufacturing company uses the term finished goods inventory. Also, instead of referring to purchases of inventory, a manufacturing company refers to the cost of goods manufactured. This means the value of goods completed and transferred to finished goods inventory during the period covered by the statement.

Computing the cost of goods manufactured is much more difficult than accounting for purchases in a merchandising company. The accountant must be able to identify all product costs and follow their flow through various manufacturing accounts. To make the task more manageable, manufacturers divide product costs into three subcategories:

1. Direct materials, which are those items purchased by a manufacturing company that go directly into the creation of what will be its finished product. For example, beef would be an item that goes into the making of a hamburger.

DIANE MANUFACTURING COMPANY
INCOME STATEMENT
FOR THE YEAR ENDED DECEMBER 31, 1989

Sales Revenues		$1,140,000
Product costs		
Finished goods inventory,		
January 1, 1989	$140,000	
Cost of goods manufactured	520,000	
Total goods available for sale	$660,000	
Finished goods inventory,		
December 31, 1989	120,000	
Cost of goods sold		540,000
Gross margin		$ 600,000
Selling and administrative expenses		
Period costs		
Salaries	$ 60,000	
Sales commissions	98,700	
Rent of sales offices	110,000	
Advertising	58,000	
Utilities	20,300	
Supplies	18,000	
Insurance	15,000	
Total selling and administrative expenses		380,000
Operating Income		$ 220,000

DIANE MANUFACTURING COMPANY
CURRENT ASSET SECTION OF THE BALANCE SHEET
DECEMBER 31, 1989

Cash	$150,000
Accounts receivable	220,000
Inventories	
Direct materials	40,000
Work in process	60,000
Finished goods	120,000
Prepaid expenses	60,000
Total Current Assets	$650,000

2. Direct labor, which encompasses the services of workers directly involved in manufacturing the product of a company. For example, the cooks in a hamburger stand prepare the hamburger for consumption, and their costs would be considered direct labor costs.

3. Manufacturing overhead, which includes those costs involved in producing a product that are not costs (such as direct materials and direct labor) that go directly into the creation of the product.

These subclassifications are used in both financial and managerial accounting.

To assign costs to products financial accountants use cost-collection techniques based on these categories. Managerial accountants recognize that the planning and control of manufacturing product costs rest with many managers in the business. For example, the foreman of a fabricating department can influence the material and labor costs in that department. But to fully control those costs, the foreman must work with the purchasing and human resources departments. The purchasing department influences the price of materials through the selection of suppliers. The human resources department influences the labor costs by establishing the labor rates. Therefore, the major task of a managerial accountant is to identify costs within the control of managers so that steps may be taken to control those costs as necessary.

MANUFACTURING COST FLOW

Figure 10-2 illustrates how these types of costs flow through the process of a company. Notice that costs move from one account to another in the same sequence as products flow through the factory to the customer. The starting point is the purchase of direct materials, recorded as an asset. As materials are used, their cost is removed from the inventory account and placed into a work-in-process account. The cost of direct material still on hand in either account at the end of the period is an asset in their respective accounts on the balance sheet.

The costs of direct labor and manufacturing overhead are treated similarly. They are recorded first in temporary accounts, then transferred to work-in-process. But unlike direct material costs, direct labor and overhead costs are recorded as they are consumed. Thus there is no ending balance in either the direct labor or the manufacturing overhead account at the balance sheet date.

As products are completed and moved from the factory to the storeroom or loading docks, the accountant moves direct material, direct labor, and manufacturing overhead costs from work-in-process to finished goods. Finally, when the products are sold their total cost is transferred from finished goods to the cost of goods sold.

This cost of goods sold account, therefore, provides the owners and/or managers with figures to compare with the sales price of goods actually sold in order to determine the gross profit generated by the business.

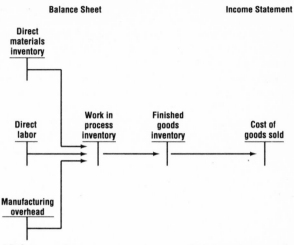

FIG. 10-2 *Manufacturing cost flows on balance sheet and income statement*

TWO PRODUCT COSTING SYSTEMS

As we dig deeper into managerial cost accounting systems, it is important to keep in mind that two basic costing procedures are used; job order cost accounting and process cost accounting.

Job order cost accounting was designed for companies whose products or services are produced in definite units to customer specification. It is the major cost accounting system used in such activities as home construction, printing, furniture, machine-tool manufacturing, management consulting, and public accounting. In all these industries, products and services differ significantly from client to client, and each job has a definite beginning and end. For example, in the home construction industry each home is built a little differently. Likewise in a printing company, the presses might be used to print an accounting book on Monday and a literary magazine on Tuesday.

It would make little sense for a building contractor to calculate an average price per house or a printing company to calculate an average cost of printing a magazine or textbook. For this reason companies providing products and services based on customer specification collect separate cost data for each job.

The cost of direct labor and manufacturing overhead are treated similarly. They are recorded first in temporary accounts, then transferred to work-in-process. But unlike direct material costs, direct labor and overhead cost are recorded as they are consumed. Thus there is no ending balance in either the direct labor or the manufacturing overhead account at the balance sheet date.

As products are completed, the accountant moves direct material, direct labor, and manufacturing overhead costs from work-in-process to finished goods. Companies providing products and services based on customer specification collect separate cost data for each job. Since costs are assigned to individual job units, such costs are calculated after each job is completed.

While job order costing is well suited to customized production, it is unsuitable for mass production of identical products. For that type of production so-called *process cost accounting* works better. Chemicals, oil refining, paint manufacturing, beer brewing, and meat packing are examples of industries that use process cost accounting.

In this system costs are accounted for by department instead of by job. Accountants generally collect these costs department by department, either weekly or monthly, to calculate the average cost per unit. At the end of an accounting period, accountants divide total costs by the number of units produced in each department. These unit costs can then be used to assign departmental costs to finished products.

Job order costing and process costing are extremes of the cost accounting systems. Few products are costed out exclusively by one method or the other. Instead, many manufacturers use a blend of the two systems, applying both at various phases of the production process. For example, an automobile manufacturer applies process costing to the production of such basic parts as shock absorbers. Engines and air-conditioning units and other components that are manufactured continuously in its parts division are also costed using process cost procedures. But finished automobiles are accounted for as separate jobs, since each must be fitted with options to meet customers' orders. Some receive air-conditioning and some AM/FM radios, whereas others require deluxe interiors. Thus the cost of each completed car off the assembly line will be different. Even when a special run of 100 identical cars is made, job order costing would be used, and the "job" would be 100 cars.

We need only reflect on the improvements in manufacturing and the "just in time" inventory system made famous in Japan to realize how sophisticated the procedures for tracing product costs have grown. ("Just-in-time inventory" is a term used for the management of the flow of inventory through a company so that it arrives only at the time it is needed to be put into the product being manufactured by the business). Over the years the use of computers has, of course, enabled business people to make determinations that would have been prohibitively expensive just a few years ago. This movement in the direction of customizing production to the customers' needs is moving managerial accounting more in the direction of being able to more precisely match costs with products. Therefore, the concept of job costing is receiving a rejuvenation in its utilization.

The change in worldwide production methods is moving the accounting treatment more in the direction of keeping precise records of the cost of goods and services. All of this also moves us in the direction of having a more precise idea of the profitability of individual products and services.

CHAPTER PERSPECTIVE

In this chapter we have begun the process of looking at the various types of costs that are incurred by a business, in order to determine how these costs can be classified in ways to help you manage your business more effectively. We have seen at the outset that there are certain costs that relate directly to the product being made and others that will be incurred by the business whether or not a product is created during the current period. We have thus seen that period costs will be incurred whether or not the company produces and sells any products and, consequently, will have to be covered by revenues in some way if the company is to avoid incurring losses in its business. We have seen that product costs, on the other hand, are those costs that go into the item the company is manufacturing. Consequently they have to be matched against the revenues from the sales of those products in order to determine when a profit (or a loss) has been generated. We have also gotten a glimpse into the way in which these costs flow through a business from the raw material stage to the finished good stage. These concepts will be important in our discussion in subsequent chapters dealing with determination of whether, in fact, the company has made a profit or a loss. With this foundation, we are now in a position to take a look at cost behavior in a more precise way.

Cost Behavior and Estimation

INTRODUCTION AND MAIN POINTS

In this chapter we will take a look at the way costs in a business relate to the behavior of the business in manufacturing products or rendering services. There are some patterns of behavior in a business that enable us to classify costs in different ways to help the business person conduct the business in a more efficient manner. In particular, this chapter will enable you to relate the level of activity being conducted by a business with the costs that will be incurred so that you can determine how well the firm is doing in generating profits or incurring losses.

After studying the material in this chapter:

━ You will have an understanding of which costs will be incurred by a company regardless of the levels of business activity that are being created (fixed costs).

━ You will have an appreciation for those costs that change in direct relation to the level of activity in the company (variable costs).

━ You will have an understanding of those costs that have certain attributes of fixed costs and variable costs (mixed costs).

━ You will have an understanding of those types of costs that remain fairly constant for certain periods of time and then change. These are called *step costs* because they step up at certain points in time; once they reach a new step level, however, they remain fixed for an additional period of time.

━ You will have an appreciation for an important concept called the *contribution format.* This is an element in managerial accounting that will enable you to determine whether a particular activity is contributing to or is a drag on, the profitability of the business as a whole.

Understanding the difference between product and period costs (previously discussed) helps managers in the planning and control of a business activity. Understanding how cost varies with changes in business activity is even more helpful. If sales volume is expected to increase, management must estimate the cost of increased inputs. To make such estimates one must first know the costs involved and the way they behave or change as activities change. Let's take a look at how this takes place.

COST BEHAVIOR PATTERNS

Not all cost varies with changes in activities, nor do those costs that vary move in the same way as other costs. To estimate expected changes in the cost, accountants must first identify the cost behavior pattern, i.e., the relationship between the cost and level of business activity. For this reason it is necessary to understand the behavior patterns for the following different types of costs:

1. Fixed costs
2. Variable costs
3. Mixed costs
4. Step costs

FIXED COSTS

Fixed costs are those whose total remains constant over a range of business activity. Within that range fixed costs can change, but not because of changes in business activity. Insurance, depreciation, and property taxes are examples of fixed costs. Other fixed costs include the expenses for administration salaries, research and development, training, and, supervisor salaries.

The range of activities over which fixed costs would not change is called the relevant range. Figure 11-1 shows depreciation cost over two relevant ranges. Notice that between zero and 40,000 units total depreciation costs are constant at $70,000. However, as production rises above 40,000 units, depreciation costs increase to $90,000. This would be because additional equipment must be purchased to achieve the higher production level.

It is important to know that, although total fixed costs remain constant in absolute terms, fixed cost *per unit* vary with the number of units produced. The more that is produced, the lower the fixed cost per unit. This is illustrated by Table 11-1.

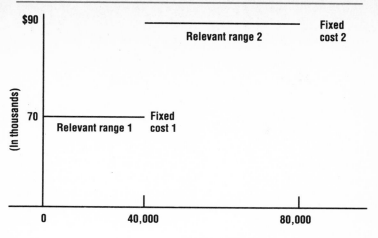

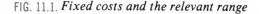

FIG. 11.1. *Fixed costs and the relevant range*

TABLE 11-1

Calculating Fixed Costs Per Unit

Number of Units Produced	Total Fixed Cost	Fixed Cost Per Unit
20,000	$70,000	$3.50
30,000	70,000	2.33
40,000	70,000	1.75

This variation in unit cost presents difficulties in both financial and managerial accounting. Assume for example that management uses fixed cost per unit in produce pricing. If 20,000 units are produced in January and 40,000 in February, should the accountant price inventory at $3.50 per unit in January and $1.75 per unit in February? Obviously, the answer is no. A consumer will not pay more for a product simply because it was produced in January. To avoid this type of stituation accountants have developed special procedures for dealing with fixed costs in order to smooth out these differences in the costing process.

VARIABLE COSTS
Variable costs are those costs whose total changes are in direct proportion to changes in business activity. Variable cost *per unit*

is constant even though activity changes. For instance, assume that production of one unit requires $3.00 of direct labor. Table 11-2 and Figure 11-2 show that total direct labor cost at three activity levels. Notice even as total cost goes up, the unit cost remains the same.

TABLE 11-2

Variable Costs

Number of Units Produced	Total Direct Labor Cost	Direct Labor Cost Per Unit
1,000	$3,000	$3.00
2,000	6,000	3.00
3,000	9,000	3.00

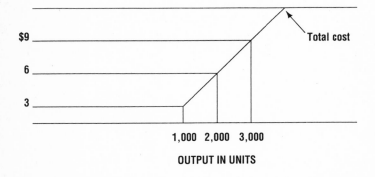

FIG. 11-2. *Variable cost behavior*

Once a business person understands the behavior pattern of each category and has an estimate of changes in business activity, he or she can estimate future costs. Notice that total cost increases in direct proportion to increases in output. This is because the variable cost per unit remains constant.

Sales commissions, and the cost of goods sold in merchandising companies are examples of variable costs. In manufacturing companies the cost of direct materials (such as parts) and direct labor (such as product assembly) are examples of variable costs for each unit produced. It is important to realize that the unit cost of direct material and direct labor remains the same. Only the total cost of these items varies, depending on the number of units produced.

MIXED COSTS

In practice many costs cannot be classified as either totally variable or totally fixed. There are combination costs that contain both variable elements and fixed elements. They are called mixed costs or semivariable costs. For example, the compensation of a sales representative who receives a base salary of $10,000 per year plus a 10 percent commission on each sales dollar he or she generates is a mixed cost.

Figure 11-3 illustrates this concept. Notice that the line representing total costs for the sales representative work starts at $10,000 on the vertical axis. This amount is a fixed part of the representative's compensation. Even if the representative does nothing, he or she would receive $10,000. The variable element, however, increases at a rate of 10% for each dollar of sales generated. Thus, if $150,000 of goods are sold, the representative's total compensation would be $25,000 ($10,000 fixed plus 10 percent times $150,000).

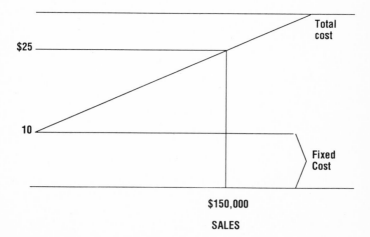

FIG. 11-3. *Mixed cost behavior*

In a manufacturing operation, electricity would be another example of mixed cost. This is because a certain amount of electricity is needed to illuminate work areas and provide security after dark. However, the cost of electricity for these purposes is fixed since the total cost does not vary with the level of the business activity. The cost of electricity for running equipment, however, does alter with changes in business activity. If sales increase, production would be stepped up, machinery would be operated for longer periods of time, and the total cost of electricity would increase.

STEP COST

Another common cost behavior pattern with which you must be familiar is the step cost. This cost is one that is fixed over a short range of activity, then increases abruptly and remains fixed over another short range. For example, supervision costs fit into this pattern. Assume, for example, that a factory is operated with one supervisor for each eight-hour shift. The number of shifts per day depends on product demand. Now assume that total production is limited to 10,000 units a month per shift and that each supervisor is paid $3,000 per month. If demand for the product is 100,000 units a month, only one shift would be needed, so that monthly supervisor cost would be $3,000. However, if demand increases to between 10,000 and 20,000 units a month, two shifts would be needed, so that supervision cost would increase (step up) to $6,000. Figure 11-4 illustrates this point.

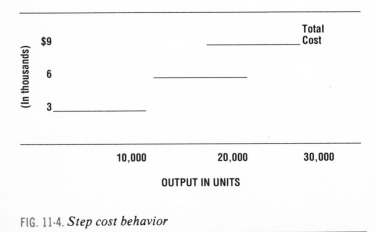

FIG. 11-4. *Step cost behavior*

COST BEHAVIOR PATTERNS

This preliminary discussion of various types of costs and their relationship to activities provides an elementary background for appreciating how managerial accounting helps to measure performance. The nature of an organization's business activity affects its cost structure. Utility companies tend to have high fixed costs because they require heavy capital investment. Manufacturing companies have high variable costs because the production process requires many raw materials and extensive labor. However, as more and more companies automate their production facilities, fixed costs are being substituted for variable costs. A good example of this would be the U.S. textile industry, which once was labor-intensive but now, because of automation, is capital intensive.

The nature of a company's business as well as the products being manufactured or sold would also affect the level of variable costs. For example, a toy manufacturer and a camera manufacturer must both decide whether to make their product out of plastic or metal. Their decision would be based both on the product design and marketability and the price of material for production.

The toy manufacturer, operating in a price-conscious market characterized by throwaway products, might well opt for the lower-priced plastic. The camera manufacturer, on the other hand, facing customer demand for quality and durability, might select a more expensive metal over plastic.

DISCRETIONARY FIXED COSTS

One other factor we must keep in mind in evaluating the relationship between costs and activity is the fact that even fixed costs have some variation to them. Depreciation costs of plant and equipment, since they are based on facilities and needs that are not easily changed, are often referred to as committed fixed costs. This is because they represent the cost of the basic facilities and the organizational structure necessary to a business. Some fixed costs, however, such as research and development and advertising, may be reduced or even eliminated over the relatively short term. These fixed costs therefore are called discretionary fixed costs, since management can partially control their level at any time. This is not saying that the elimination of research and development or advertising would be a good long-term business decision, but in terms of a short-term need for cost-cutting, they can be controlled.

THE CONTRIBUTION FORMAT

Once total costs have been separated into fixed and variable categories, how do managerial accountants use that information in monitoring a business? One important use involves the construction of a special income statement that differs from the functional income statement we have seen in earlier chapters. These statements are referred to as functional income statements because they group expenses by business function, such as production, selling, and administrative. Let's compare that, however, with a format called the contribution format income statement set forth in Table 11-3.

TABLE 11-3
COMPARISON OF THE FUNCTIONAL INCOME STATEMENT WITH A CONTRIBUTION INCOME STATEMENT

A. Functional Income Statement

Sales revenue	$955,000
Cost of goods sold	597,500
Gross margin	$357,500
Selling & administrative expenses	276,000
Operating income	81,500

B. Contribution Income Statement

Sales revenue		$955,000
Variable cost		
Cost of goods sold	$477,500	
Selling & administrative expenses	191,000	668,500
Contribution margin		$286,500
Fixed expenses		
Manufacturing	$120,000	
Operating	85,000	205,000
Operating income		$ 81,500

Note how variable expenses are first deducted from sales revenue to obtain what accountants call the contribution margin. Next, fixed expenses are deducted from the contribution margin to obtain operating income. This contribution income statement has expenses grouped by cost behavior rather than business function.

The contribution margin is a crucial figure because it tells management the amount of sales contributed toward fixed expenses and toward operating income. This contribution format is used extensively in business for internal planning and control. It is useful in analyzing cost-volume-profit relationships as well as product profitability and sales and managerial performance. It therefore sets the stage for a more in-depth discussion of these subjects in subsequent chapters.

CHAPTER PERSPECTIVE

In this chapter we have introduced you to the fixed and variable aspects of cost in a company and their implications for determining profitability. We have seen that many costs are not absolutely fixed or totally variable. Rather, both types of cost have aspects that are constant over certain periods of time and varied over other periods of time. It is important that you have an understanding of these elements in the cost of your business if you are truly going to be in a position to determine whether you are making money or losing money as your business activity changes. In this chapter, also, we have given you an introduction to the contribution concept, which essentially is the determination of the extent to which a particular product line or service activity is meeting or exceeding its variable costs. The excess of revenues over variable costs provides a contribution margin, which will help you pay the fixed costs that will be burdening the company whether or not a particular business activity takes place. With this foundation, now it is time to take a look at the way in which the level of activity in a business impacts cost and profit.

Cost-Volume-Profit Analysis

INTRODUCTION AND MAIN POINTS

In this chapter we are going to start to use the tools we acquired in Chapter 11 and see to what extent the management of a business or division of a business can be conducted more efficiently through cost/volume/profit analysis. While the term might sound somewhat foreboding, essentially all it means is there are different levels of profit (or loss) that a company can expect depending on the level of business activity it is conducting.

After studying the material in this chapter:

■ You will know how a break-even point is computed in the company to determine at what level you must operate in order to at least have no loss, even though you may have no profit.

■ You will have an understanding of what levels of activity you must reach in order to achieve certain target profit levels that you have set.

■ You will see how to establish margins of safety so that you know how much you can increase or decrease a firm's business activity and still fall within a certain range of profit.

■ You will have an understanding of how price change decisions for your products will impact the determination of your profitability in the future. Also you will see to what extent increases or decreases in profit will result from increases or decreases in business volume.

■ You will be able to utilize the knowledge of changes in variable costs and fixed costs to determine what impact they will have on the profitability of your business.

■ You will have a preliminary exposure to the way cost/volume/profit analysis changes when a company makes more than one product and has costs attributable to the various products created.

The key factor in almost any business decision-making is the effect on the organization's profits. Managerial accountants are expected to answer such questions as:

1. How would a 5-percent increase in sales price affect profits?
2. If variable manufacturing costs are reduced 7 percent, how many units of product must be sold to earn $100,000 profit?
3. If an airline offers a special fare between New York and Miami, how would the revenue, cost, and profits change?
4. If a fast-food company increases its advertising budget by $1,000,000, how many hamburgers must it sell to cover the increase in this expense?
5. If a bookstore extends its hours, how much additional revenue must it earn to cover the increased operating expenses?

The answers to these questions require that we look at the cost-volume-profit analysis. This is a method of estimating how changes in the following variables will affect profit: unit variable cost, unit sales price, total fixed cost per period, sales volume, and sales mix. ("Sales mix" means the amount of sales of different products that a business enters into during a given period.) As the name implies, cost-volume-profit analysis is an examination of how total revenue and total cost (and therefore profit) vary with changes in sales volume.

BASIC ASSUMPTIONS

Cost-volume-profit analysis is based on a number of assumptions, such as:

1. A firm's total revenue changes in direct proportion to changes in its unit sales volume.
2. Total costs can be separated into fixed and variable costs.
3. Total variable costs change in direct portion to changes in sales volume. That is, the average variable cost per unit remains constant over some relevant range.
4. Total fixed costs remain constant over the range of sales volume being considered.
5. Sales mix remains the same over the range of sales volume being considered.
6. Sales volume equals production volume; that is, inventory levels remain constant.

Cost-volume-profit analysis can be done either mathematically or graphically. This book is not geared to go into this in detail. Suffice it to say at this point that a mathematical equation approach starts with the simple equation:

Sales revenue − variable cost − fixed cost = profit

This allows the business person to determine changes in results based on the alterations of key variables.

Contribution margin per unit is the dollar amount contributed by the sale of unit to fixed cost. After covering variable cost, the sale contributes to the company's operating income. We discussed in an earlier chapter the per-unit variable cost and per-unit fixed cost and how alterations in sales volume and in sales price per unit can impact on profitability.

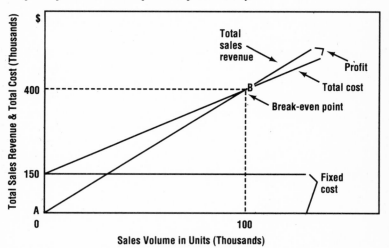

FIG. 12-1. *Cost-volume-profit graph*

From a graphic standpoint a cost-volume-profit graph can show the relationship between revenue-cost-profit and volume over a wide range of sales activity. The graphic approach is illustrated in Figure 12-1. This cost-volume-profit graph illustrates the relationship between sales volume and revenues and between sales volume and cost. The difference between the total cost and total revenue lines is the profit or loss at each sales level. The break-even point is the point at which the total revenue line and total cost line intersect.

MANAGERIAL USES OF COST-VOLUME-PROFIT ANALYSIS

Since we have a rudimentary understanding of cost-volume-profit analysis, let's explore some examples of how this analysis enables business people to gather information for managerial planning and decision-making. First of all, you can calculate the sales volume needed to achieve a specific profit. You can also determine how a change in price, sales volume, variable cost, or fixed cost affects profit. Furthermore, you can estimate the acceptable range between expected sales volume and break-even sales volume. Let's take a look at a few examples.

TARGET PROFIT CASE

After making an investment in a project or business, the investor expects to receive some level of profit; this is often referred to as the target profit. Cost-volume-profit analysis can be used to determine the number of units that must be sold or sales dollars that must be earned for a company to achieve its target profit. Suppose we assume the basic figures for the company acquired are:

sales price $4.00 per unit; variable cost $2.50 per unit; fixed cost $150,000 per year.

Assume the owners invested $200,000 in the company and desire a 25 percent annual return on their investment. This means that the company has a target profit of $50,000 (25% × $200,000 = $50,000). To determine the number of units that must be sold to earn this profit, substitute the required profit of $50,000 into the cost-volume-profit equation and then calculate the number of sales units as follows:

Sales revenue	=	variable cost + fixed cost + profit.
$4.00 X	=	$2.50 × X + ($150,000 + $50.000)
$1.50 X	=	$200,000
X	=	$133,333.

MARGIN OF SAFETY CASE

Sometimes management wants to know the amount actual sales volume can drop before its company will incur a loss. Called the "margin of safety," this amount is the difference between the expected sales volume and the break-even point in units divided by expected sales volume. Generally expressed as a percentage of expected sales volume, it is computed as follows:

$$\text{Margin of safety} = \frac{\text{Expected sales volume - Break-even sales volume}}{\text{Expected sales volume}}$$

Assume Walsh Company's expected sales are 133,333 units and its break-even point is 100,000 units. Walsh's margin of safety is 25 percent. That is, if actual sales drop to 25 percent below expected sales volume, the firm will only break even.

Managers use this margin of safety to indicate the risk inherent in a sales plan. The larger the margin, the less the risk. If the planned margin of safety is unacceptably low, management will consider increasing sales activity or decreasing costs to improve the margin.

PRICE CHANGE CASE

Managers must constantly decide whether to change sales prices. Consumers tend to resist price increases by buying less of a product, which can offset the effect of a price increase on profits. Sometimes competition forces management to consider a price reduction. Using cost-volume-profit analysis, the business person can determine the sales volume that must be maintained after instituting a price change in order to yield the target profit.

Assume that the Walsh Company is considering a price increase of $0.25 per unit. How many units must be sold at the new price to break even? To achieve a $50,000 profit? The computations, when cost-volume-profit analysis is used, are shown below:

	Original Data	$0.25 Increase in Sales Price
Sales price per unit	$ 4.00	$ 4.25
Variable cost per unit	2.50	2.50
Contribution margin per unit	$ 1.50	$ 1.75
Total fixed costs	$ 150,000	$ 150,000
Target profit	50,000	50,000
Break-even sales units =	$ 150,000	$ 150,000
	$ 1.50	$ 1.75
	=100,000	= 85,714
Sales units to earn a $50,000 target profit	$ 200,000	$ 200,000
	$ 1.50	$ 1.75
	=133,333	=114,286

These computations indicate that a $0.25 increase in sales price would reduce the break-even point from 100,000 units to 85,714 units. The number of units that must be sold to earn a $50,000 profit has been reduced from 133,333 to 114,286 units.

Should the Walsh Company increase its sales price? The answer depends on whether management thinks the company can sell 114,286 units at $4.25 per unit as easily as it can sell 133,333 units at $4.00 per unit. If the price is raised, Walsh can sustain a 19,047 decrease in sales volume (133,333 − 114,286) and still earn a $50,000 profit. If sales decline less than 19,047 units, profits will exceed $50,000.

EFFECT OF CHANGE IN VARIABLE COSTS

Some business environments do not always allow business people to increase sales prices. Competition may be too strong, for one thing. In such cases one option is to decrease costs rather than increase sales prices. Costs can often be reduced by using less expensive materials, by installing labor-saving equipment, or by purchasing materials in bulk at quantity discounts. To estimate the effect of these cost reductions, you must again use cost-volume-profit analysis.

Assume Walsh Company has the opportunity to reduce variable costs by $0.20 per unit by purchasing in bulk. Also assume that Walsh's target profit remains at $50,000. How many units must Walsh sell to break even? to earn a $50,000 profit? The computations are as follows:

	Original Data	$0.20 Decrease in Variable Costs
Sales price per unit	$ 4.00	$ 4.00
Variable costs per unit	2.50	2.30
Contribution margin per unit	$ 1.50	$ 1.70
Total fixed costs	$150,000	$150,000
Target profit	50,000	50,000
Break-even sales units =	$150,000	$150,000
	$ 1.50	$ 1.70
	= 100,000	= 88,235
Sales units to earn a $50,000 target profit	$200,000	$200,000
	$ 1.50	$ 1.70
	= 133,333	= 117,647

The decrease in variable costs of $0.20 per unit reduces the break-even point from 100,000 units to 88,235 units. The number of units that must be sold to earn a $50,000 profit is reduced from 133,333 to 117,647 units.

EFFECT OF A CHANGE IN FIXED COST

Generally, fixed costs are not expected to change during the year. In the annual planning process, however, business people must reassess the company's level of discretionary fixed costs (i.e., costs that can be changed in a relatively short time frame) in light of ever-changing business conditions.

For example, business managers can increase fixed cost items, such as advertising or research and development, in order to increase sales volume or to develop new products for the future, or they might decrease training costs in order to raise the current year's operating profit. Any increase or decrease in fixed expenses changes the break-even point and the sales volume necessary to achieve a target profit.

Assume the manager of O'Connor Company is considering a $20,000 increase in advertising expenditures. How many units must be sold to break even given this cost increase? to earn a profit of $50,000?

The $20,000 increase in fixed cost increases the break-even sales volume by 13,333 units and raises the sales volume needed to achieve the target profit by 13,334 units.

Should the O'Connor Company increase its advertising expenditures? That depends on the additional sales volume to be realized from the additional cost. If the new advertising is expected to increase sales volume by at least 13,333 units, O'Connor Company should buy the additional advertising.

SIMULTANEOUS PRICE AND COST CHANGES

Thus far we have only considered changes in one variable at a time. In reality, prices and costs often change at the same time. Variable costs change frequently, and business people react by changing their prices. Using the O'Connor example, assume that managers are considering a $20,000 increase in advertising costs. They hope to cover this increased cost by raising sales prices by $0.25 per unit. How many units does O'Connor have to sell to break even? to earn a $50,000 profit? The answers are worked out in the following example.

The increase in the sales price of $0.25 coupled with the added $20,000 fixed expense reduces the break-even point to 97,143 units. It also reduces the number of units that must be sold to earn the target profit to 125,714 units.

Should management implement the proposed changes? Again, that depends on their expectations for sales volume, which of course cannot be forecast with complete accuracy. If O'Connor can sell 125,714 units or more at a price of $4.25, then the expected profit would be greater than $50,000. But if the increased price is likely to lower demand below 125,714, units the proposal should not be implemented.

MULTIPRODUCT COST VOLUME PROFIT ANALYSIS

Up to this point we have been dealing with cost-volume-profit analysis in a company that produces only one product. Under these circumstances the major factors to be considered are sales price, variable costs, fixed costs, and sales volume of a single product. When cost-volume-profit analysis is applied to a multiproduct firm, managers must consider the price, cost, and sales volume of each product. But the firm's overall profitability also depends on the sales mix, sometimes called the product mix. This is the proportion of sales volume contributed by each product. For example, if a firm sells 40,000 units of product A and 60,000 units of product B, its sales mix is 40 percent A and 60 percent B. Sales mix is important because the contribution margins of products often differ.

Analysis of this complexity is beyond the level of this book. However, it should be noted that computers have now enabled business people to make calculations of this type in a fairly rapid manner. Computer programs of this type can quickly calculate the impact of change in price, cost and volume on an organization's profits. To answer such "What if" questions as those listed in the beginning of this chapter, many companies use interactive programs of basic cost-volume-profit equations on their microcomputers to analyze data on a real time basis as they are collected. These programs interactive capabilities allow managers to enter and change their inputs easily and also make the analysis of the financial effects of various alternatives simpler. Some examples of the type of software available to the public are set forth in the following list:

Accountants Microsystems
ADP Software
AJV Computerized Data
   Management
Alpine Data
APS Pension Services
Best Programs
Centerpiece Software
CP Aid Software
Creative Solutions
Datacopy
Interactive Systems

Kelly PC-PRO
Lexis Tax Database
Matthew Bender Tax Source
NARS (National Accounting
   Research System)
Nexis Accounting Database
Phinet Tax Database
Ryan Software
Sawitney Software
Tax Ease
Time Express
Westlaw Tax Database

CHAPTER PERSPECTIVE

In this chapter we have exposed you to the way in which variations in business activity can result in different levels of profit or loss in the business. You have gained an appreciation for how the amount of fixed and variable costs in your business can impact your reaching a break-even point or a target profit level. Equally important, you have seen the way in which pricing decisions in your business can be impacted by the structure of the costs in your business, thereby putting you in a position of evaluating the extent to which a reduction in prices may increase your profits or, on the other hand, how increases in prices might reduce your profits—all conditional on the fixed and variable cost structure of your business. And finally, you have gotten a preliminary exposure to the fact that, the more products you add to your product line, the more you will be required to determine what types of costs relate to the various types of products you are producing and selling if you are to maintain the profit levels you desire.

Budgeting

INTRODUCTION AND MAIN POINTS

In this chapter we are going to look into the future of your business and help you plan for it. The concept is called budgeting. Up to this point we have been talking more from an historical perspective in our discussion of the various types of costs involved in conducting a business. That was certainly true in financial accounting and, while less true, still was a part of our discussion of managerial accounting up to this point. Now that we have under our belts an understanding of the way costs relate to business activity, we can start talking about making some projections into the future.

After studying the material in this chapter:

▬ You will have an understanding as to how your estimates of future sales will enable you to create a sales budget for your business for the year to come.

▬ You will be able to relate to that sales budget the amount of goods you will have to produce or services you'll have to render during the current period in order to meet those sales budgets. This will enable you to create a production budget that will outline the costs likely to be incurred in order to meet the production levels you have set.

▬ You will understand how to develop a budget for your selling expenses and administrative expenses based on this sales budget. Although selling and administrative expenses are not as directly related to sales as the production budget, they are nevertheless important in giving you an idea of the total costs involved in meeting sales targets.

▬ You will be able to develop from the foregoing items a budgeted income statement that will be your blueprint for the year to come in terms of measuring the extent to which the firm is on the course toward meeting profit objectives.

■ You will have an appreciation for how this budgeted income statement relates to the company's cash flow, which is the source of financing the business activity that you have targeted.

There is a saying that if you want to get from New York to Chicago, it's essential that you know where Chicago is! That is, if you're serious about achieving something, you must sooner or later establish a goal and a plan to reach it. Without such direction you have no clear basis on which to make day-to-day decisions. Business managers face this type of problem all the time. They must develop a plan to guide them in their decision-making. In this chapter we will see how projected data on revenues and costs can be used to develop such a plan, which is called a *budget*. The budget involves putting numbers on the marketing, production, and financial plans that are used to establish goals for revenues, expenses, assets, liabilities, and other business activities. The budget consists of a series of documents that communicate expected results of operations to managers at all levels and in all business functions. Periodically the budget is used to compare actual results of operations with forecast results to see how well managers have met established goals.

The master budget is a series of interrelated budgets that quantify top management's expectations about revenue, expenses, net income, cash flows, and financial position. The details in financial terms indicate how the company will achieve its goals and objectives for the coming year. The master budget consists of an income budget, a budgeted balance sheet, and a cash budget.

Generally a lot of time and effort on the part of all members of an organization is needed to prepare a master budget. Many times managers complain that they are too busy to prepare a budget. Yet, on closer examination, we find that managers who make such comments are usually taking actions based on some implicit budget plans. They are always trying to anticipate what will happen next, then to prepare for it. In fact, most managers have fairly well-defined ideas about what they want to accomplish and how they want to do it. Budgeting merely formalizes those ideas, enabling managers to communicate their ideas to others.

There are four major advantages to a master budget:
1. It helps in implementing a business plan efficiently and effectively and in achieving a business's objectives.
2. It coordinates activities among various segments of a business.

3. It provides a means of communicating the plan throughout the business.
4. It provides a standard for evaluating the performance of the firm's manager's (perhaps this is the real reason why some managers don't like budgets.)

AN OVERVIEW OF THE MASTER BUDGET

The master budget is made up of two major parts: the operating budget and the financial budget. The operating budget represents the expected results of operations and contains the following elements:

1. Sales budget
2. Production budget
   a. Direct materials budget
   b. Direct labor budget
   c. Manufacturing overhead budget.
3. Ending inventory budget.
4. Selling and administrative expense budget.
5. Budgeted income statement.

Note the similarity to the captions in the income statement we discussed in Chapter 6.

The financial budget details capital expenditures and summarizes how operations affect the company's cash balances and expected financial position. The financial budget contains:

1. Capital expenditure budget
2. Cash budget
3. Budgeted balance sheet

All of the above are strongly interrelated and must be prepared before the master budget can be finalized. In order to better understand these interrelationships, there is set forth in Figure 13-1 a diagram of the way in which the master budget relationships work together.

The sales budget is the starting point for the whole process because all of the other budgets depend on sales for their very existence. Based on the forecast sales for the coming year, the sales budget has a cause-and-effect relationship with the selling and administrative expense budget. This is because a certain level of sales depends primarily on the amount of money available for advertising and promotion.

Once the sales budget is established, a production budget for expected sales volumes can be developed. This budget determines the direct material, direct labor, and manufacturing overhead budgets. All three of these budgets feed into the budgeted income statement, which is then used to prepare the financial budgets.

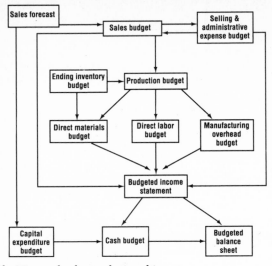

FIG. 13-1. *Master budget relationships*

The capital expenditure budget lists all approved long-range expenditures needed to improve the firm's capacity or long-range efficiency. It is based on the sales forecast as well as other information. Both the budgeted capital expenditures and the budgeted income information are then used to prepare the budgeted balance sheet.

Budgets are used for planning and control decisions during the fiscal year. In the past, only major economic changes would cause a company to change a budget once it was established. At the end of the fiscal year a new budget was prepared for the coming year.

An alternative to this traditional budgeting approach is the continuous budget: sometimes called a rolling budget. The continuous budget is revised at the end of each quarter and adds one new quarter. Thus the new, revised budget covers the next three quarters plus one additional quarter. The major advantage of a continuous budget is that it makes planning a continual activity.

To illustrate the step-by-step development of the master budget, let us follow the process of Fordham Corporation. Fordham produces and sells a single product—desks—in a single facility. The cost of production includes direct materials, direct labor, and manufacturing overhead. (The work-in-process inventory will be considered negligible and is omitted from this discussion.)

CASE STUDY

Based on engineering studies, product specifications, and managerial estimates, the following unit cost estimates for direct materials, direct labor, and variable overhead were compiled by Fordham's accountants:

Direct materials *equal* 1 lb. of material per unit *times* $2.00 per pound equals = $2.00 per unit.

Direct labor required equals 1 quarter-hour of labor *times* $20.00 per hour = $5.00 per unit.

Variable overhead *equals* 80 percent of the direct labor dollar *times* $5.00 per unit = $4.00 per unit.

The direct materials budget involves three parts:
1. A usage budget, which estimates the quantity and cost of direct materials needed to meet current production requirements.
2. A purchase budget, which estimates the quantity and cost of direct material purchases that are needed for production and to maintain acceptable inventory levels.
3. An expected cash payment schedule, which shows cash outflows for direct material purchases that are usually made on credit.

The direct materials budget for the Fordham Corporation is shown on the next page.

The direct labor budget is a statement showing the quantity, cost, and period of payment for labor that can be directly identified with specific products. The direct labor budget is used to plan the size of the work force needed for production requirements.

Finally, the manufacturing overhead budget summarizes all expected manufacturing costs other than direct labor cost as well as expected cash payments for these costs. This budget is based on overhead costs being classified as variable or fixed and on the relationship of variable costs to a suitable activity measure such as direct labor dollars.

The ending inventory budget is a statement showing the cost of ending direct materials, work-in-process, and finished goods inventory. This budget is used to prepare the balance sheet at the end of each budget.

FORDHAM CORPORATION
DIRECT MATERIALS BUDGET
FOR THE YEAR ENDED DECEMBER 31, 1987

	Quarter 1	Quarter 2	Quarter 3	Quarter 4	Year
Schedule 1: Usage Budget					
Unit production requirements	$58,000	$55,500	$46,500	$50,000	$210,000 [1]
Direct materials required per unit of output (pounds) . .	× 1	× 1	× 1	× 1	× 1
Direct materials required (pounds)	58,000	55,500	46,500	50,000	210,000 [2]
Cost per pound of material	× $2	× $2	× $2	× $2	× $2
Total cost of direct materials required	$116,000	$111,000	$93,000	$100,000	$420,000
Schedule 2: Purchases Budget					
Direct materials required (pounds)	58,000	55,500	46,500	50,000	210,000 [3]
Add estimated ending direct materials inventory (pounds)	+ 5,550	+ 4,650	+ 5,000	+ 5,000	+ 5,000 [4]
Total direct materials required	63,550	60,150	51,500	55,000	215,000
Less beginning direct materials inventory	− 5,000	− 5,550	− 4,650	− 5,000	− 5,000 [5]
Direct materials purchase requirements (pounds)	58,000	54,600	46,850	50,000	210,000
Cost per pound of material	× $2	× $2	× $2	× $2	× $2 [6]
Total cost of direct materials purchases	$117,000	$109,200	$93,700	$100,000	$420,000

Source of Data:
1. *Management's estimates*
2. *Management's estimates*
3. *See above*
4. *Management's estimates: 10% x direct materials required in next quarter*
5. *Estimating ending direct materials inventory for last quarter*
6. *Management's estimates*

Schedule 3: Expected Cash Payments for Purchases

	Quarter 1	Quarter 2	Quarter 3	Quarter 4	Year
Accounts payable	$ 50,000				$ 50,000
Purchases: Quarter 1	81,970	$ 35,130			117,100[7]
Quarter 2		76,440	$32,760		109,200[8]
Quarter 3			65,590	$ 28,110	93,700[9]
Quarter 4				70,000	70,000[10]
Total cash payments for purchases	$131,970	$111,570	$98,350	$ 98,110	$440,000

Source of Data:

7. *Management's estimates: 70% in quarter of purchase; 30% in following quarter*
8. *Management's estimates: 70% in quarter of purchase; 30% in following quarter*
9. *Management's estimates: 70% in quarter of purchase; 30% in following quarter*
10. *Management's estimates: 70% in quarter of purchase; 30% in following quarter.*

SELLING AND ADMINISTRATIVE EXPENSE BUDGET

The selling and administrative budget is a detailed listing of nonmanufacturing expenses during a budget period as well as expected cash payments for these expenditures. Business people separate variable and fixed expenses in making this determination. Variable expenses generally include such items as sales commissions, travel and entertainment, clerical services, and shipping expenses. By analyzing past expenses and adjusting them for inflation and other anticipated changes, accountants can estimate each variable expense as a percent of each sales dollar.

BUDGETED INCOME STATEMENT

The budgeted income statement shows estimated revenues and expenses from profit-directed activities for a specific accounting period. The budgeted income statement summarizes the information from the sales, manufacturing, and selling and administrative expense budgets discussed earlier. Thus, all these operating budgets feed into the budgeted income statement. The purpose of the budgeted income statement is to estimate the company's after-tax income.

CASH BUDGET

The cash budget is a period-by-period statement of the following items:

1. Cash on hand at the start of a budget period
2. Expected cash receipts
3. Expected cash disbursements
4. The resulting cash balance at the end of the budget period

The cash budget summarizes cash receipts and expenditures. It helps identify periods in which a company might need extra cash, so loans can be negotiated in a timely manner. In fact, banks require businesses to plan their cash needs carefully. Businesses that make urgent, last-minute loan requests must generally pay higher interest rates. The cash budget also helps identify periods in which a company may have more cash than necessary. Excess cash can be invested in short-term securities to earn additional income.

BUDGETED BALANCE SHEET

The budgeted balance sheet is an estimate of a firm's financial position at the end of the budget period. It is developed from previous budgets, with beginning balances adjusted to include any changes in assets, liabilities, and equity planned for in the operating and financial budgets.

USE OF COMPUTERIZED FINANCIAL PLANNING MODELS

The budgeting process described above and the resulting master budget do not always produce a plan acceptable to management. Sometimes managers must adjust their estimates, which means changing many of the budget documents.

If the budget is prepared using a computer, such changes can be made easily. For example, where a master budget was prepared using a spreadsheet program on a microcomputer, data from the company's year-end balance sheet and estimates for the new year can be entered into the spreadsheet along with formulas for the interrelationship of the various budgets. The computer then can calculate and print out the complete master budget. To find the effect of an estimate, such as the percentage of sales collected or the cost of material, the business person simply enters the change and the computer recalculates the budget amounts and prints out a new budget. Managers can therefore see the effect of the change on all components of the master budget immediately.

All sound businesses have a need for some type of future planning. To prepare and evaluate such plans is a demanding exercise of many business skills. The budgeting process is the expression in financial terms of the management's thinking. Budgeting is important in that it makes managers and owners set forth in specific terms what they may have in vague terms in their own minds. The process of budgeting also is helpful in that it sometimes discloses to the business person areas that weren't thought of when the business was being conducted in a more subjective way. Consequently, this part of accounting is most helpful to the business person. It helps him or her think through how the ideas for generating profits are going to be carried out in specific terms.

CHAPTER PERSPECTIVE

In this chapter we have seen how we put together individual budgets, which ultimately culminate in what might be called a master budget or a master blueprint for the company in the future. Budgets can be for one month, one year, or a longer period of time. The purpose of the budget is not to constrain a company from expansion but rather to enable business people to see the overall implications of a change in business activity. We have seen that a budget need not be a straitjacket; it is a flexible plan that can be changed with changing conditions as business activity is carried forward. Now that we have a feeling for the way in which accounting can be used in creating plans for the business, how can accounting be used for seeing that those plans actually are met? That is the subject for the next chapter.

Relevance of Costs to Management Decisions

INTRODUCTION AND MAIN POINTS

In the last chapter you had the opportunity of working on the creation of a budget to guide the activity of your business. Accounting is also a powerful tool in areas beyond creating plans; it can also be useful in seeing that those plans are properly carried forward. Therefore, in this chapter we are going to take a look at how costs are relevant to the decisions made by management in order to meet the plans we discussed in Chapter 13.

After studying the material in this chapter:

■ You will be in a position to see how management decisions have an impact on the financial results of a business.

■ You will see how business decisions and the results from them interrelate with the budgets that have been set for the business during the time period involved.

■ You will know how accounting can be used in helping you decide whether you should make or buy specific components for your products.

■ You will have an understanding of how accounting can help you determine whether you should add a product or drop a product from your product line when you think that doing so will enhance your profitability.

■ You will have an appreciation of the way joint products and by-products result from your main production activity and how to determine the costs of the company that are related to the various products that result from your operations.

Business managers must constantly make decisions and determine not only what products the company should produce, but also how much of each product should be scheduled for production. There are many other questions, too, such as, from which suppliers should the company order its materials? In addition, managers must estimate how each decision they make will affect operating income. The managerial accountant's role in this process is to supply information on changes in costs and revenues to facilitate the decision process.

To this point we have seen how costs and volume relate to profit analysis. We've also had the opportunity to see the rudimentary points of budget planning. These have all been examined in the context of decisions that come up regularly. But what about managerial decisions of a nonrecurring nature? For example:

1. A discount house will place a large order with the manufacturer if its normal selling price is reduced. Should the order be accepted?

2. A company has been purchasing a part from an outside supplier. Because some of the purchaser's facilities have become idle, it could fabricate the part itself. Should the company make or continue to buy the part?

3. A major company engages in both food processing and toy manufacturing. The company's directors are dissatisfied with recent performance, so they are considering selling the toy business. Would the company be better off without the toy division?

4. A refining company's processing network produces several intermediate products. Should the company sell all the products "as is" or process some further?

Nonrecurring decisions of this type present opportunities, often unexpected, for management to improve a firm's profitability. Managerial accounting plays a vital role in helping managers meet the challenge of these special decisions.

Let us take a look at a few situations where these types of opportunities arise and how they might be handled.

SPECIAL ORDERS

Quite often companies anticipating future increases in the number of their customers construct new manufacturing facilities. Such investments are usually well advised even if these firms will have excess capacity for a few years. Building only for current needs means haphazard expansion, which can be more expensive in the long run than planned investments. Another common cause of excess capacity is the transfer of production to foreign countries to take advantage of lower wage scales. Many manufacturers import products, leaving U.S. factories underutilized.

In these types of cases managers may be asked to consider accepting a special order for their product at a reduced price to make use of the excess or idle facilities. Such orders are worth considering providing they will not affect regular sales of the same product. To decide whether an order will be profitable at a lower price, business managers must isolate its relevant costs.

Looking at such factors as (1) the impact of the special order on the sales of existing products and (2) the impact of the additional production on both fixed and variable costs of the existing products, will help the manager determine whether the special order will increase the contribution margin and operating income of the company.

In connection with special orders of this type, one must also consider whether fixed costs will truly remain fixed. Spreading the fixed cost over additional units of production will produce a lower fixed unit cost for the company's regular line of products. On the other hand, if the special order pushes up step costs of the type we discussed earlier, it might ratchet up the fixed costs to a new (and higher) level, and this would be a detriment to the company. Thus, in evaluating such nonrecurring decisions for special orders, business people must be careful to base their calculations on *total* unit fixed costs.

"MAKE OR BUY" DECISIONS

The make or buy decision is a management decision about whether an item should be made internally or bought from an outside supplier. To put idle capacity to use, firms often consider manufacturing parts or subassemblies of the part they are currently purchasing. For example, a manager of an automobile manufacturer might use idle capacity to manufacture spark plugs instead of buying them from an outside supplier. Or a company that manufactures refrigerators might fabricate its own electronic components instead of importing them from Europe.

When these opportunities arise, the managerial accountant is often asked to compare the cost of manufacturing a part internally with the cost of purchasing it.

ADDING AND DROPPING PRODUCTS

Over time, consumer preferences change. Some products become obsolete and are dropped from product lines. Others are developed to replace them. An important factor in deciding whether to add or drop a product is the decision's effect on operating income. Again, relevant costs are the key to the business person's analysis.

For example, consider the case of a drugstore that carries three product lines: drugs, general merchandise, and cosmetics. Suppose cosmetics sales show a net loss. Given the loss on this product, the owners think it should be dropped. Perhaps the first question the accountant should ask is, which fixed expenses are associated with that product line and which are avoidable? An avoidable cost is a cost that can be eliminated by ceasing some economic activity or by improving the efficiency with which that activity is carried out. For cosmetics, avoidable fixed expenses might include the salaries of employees assigned to that department and advertising expenses specific to that line. Unavoidable costs would include such fixed expenses as the store manager's salary, rent, and utilities. These costs are not relevant to the determination because they would continue regardless of whether the line was kept or dropped.

Taking these types of factors into account, the accountant could determine that dropping the cosmetic line would eliminate all the sales but not all the costs attributable to that particular line of product; consequently, it could have a detrimental effect on the store's overall net income.

JOINT PRODUCTS AND BY-PRODUCTS

In some industries several products are produced from one material. For example, the cracking of crude oil yields gasoline, kerosene, heating oil, and other oil-base products. Although the relative proportions can be changed by altering how the crude oil is processed, none can be entirely eliminated. Products made from a common input are often referred to as joint products or by-products. In an analysis of this type, the point in the manufacturing process at which a product is identifiable and can be separately processed or sold is called the split-off point. Costs incurred before the split-off point benefit all products and are called *joint costs*. Costs incurred after the split-off point for the benefit of only one product are called *separable costs*. For example, in lumber processing the costs of the trees are joint costs. Once the trees have been processed into separate products, the direct labor and overhead needed to finish processing them are considered separable costs. An example of this is set forth in Figure 14-1. In this illustration, costs incurred before the split-off point are joint costs for rough-sawing the trees into planks and beams. Costs incurred after the split-off point are separable costs traceable to a single product.

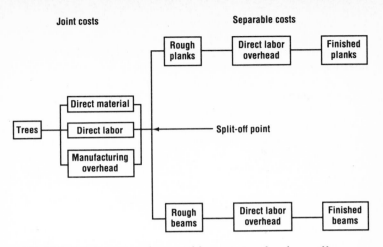

FIG. 14-1 *Joint costs and separable costs in a lumber mill*

This example summarizes the relationship of joint costs and separable costs. Once materials have been split between the products, a manager must decide whether to market each product as is or process it further. The question in this sell-or-process-further decision is whether the additional cost of processing can be justified by the greater revenues earned. For example, will the added revenue from selling leather gloves cover the expense of making gloves from the cowhides rather than selling the hides to shoe manufacturers? The answer to this question depends upon market conditions. If the demand for leather gloves rises or falls, managers would have to reevaluate their decision.

The foregoing management decisions are, as we can see, significantly impacted by the costs that are relevant to the operations involved. The examples given are but a few of the types of alternatives that businesses face today.

The advent of the microcomputer and appropriate software has enabled companies to make relatively sophisticated computations based on all the factors involved here, providing even small entrepreneurial organizations with the capability of making decisions of this type.

CHAPTER PERSPECTIVE

In this chapter we have begun to look at how cost/volume/profit analysis impacts on your decisions as a business person. We have seen that your decision to make or buy a product, to add or drop a product line, or to accept or reject a special order for products can be based on whether or not such moves are likely to enhance the profitability of the company. We have also seen that there are very often different types of products that emanate from a firm's production process. Costs follow all of these types of products in different ways. As a result your decision process with regard to whether or not you have a profitable product is also impacted by what you've learned in this chapter. Now that you have seen how accounting helps a firm's managers set goals for the future through budgeting and helps evaluate the effects of managerial decisions, it is time that you take a look at how to measure the performance of a firm's managers and employees in meeting those goals.

Responsibility Accounting

INTRODUCTION AND MAIN POINTS

In this chapter we will expand on your ability to evaluate the behavior of a firm's employees by using responsibility accounting. In prior chapters we have focused on how accounting is used to set plans for the business as a whole. Now the question is, how does one measure the performance of employees once those plans have been put in place? We have seen in Chapter 14 that business people must make informed decisions in order to implement plans for business profitability. Once those decisions are made, however, management must also follow up in order to determine how the plans are implemented and to measure the results achieved by the firm's employees.

After studying the material in this chapter:

— You will understand the concepts of responsibility accounting, which is the use of accounting to measure the performance of business people.

— You will know the basic functions by which performance is measured—production, marketing, finance, and human resources.

— You will be familiar with the various types of centers in the company for which responsibility has to be measured—expense centers, revenue centers, profit centers, and investment centers.

— You will understand the various types of costs that are attributable to these various centers and the way in which they lead to performance measurement.

— You will be exposed to the way in which costs are assigned to inventory, which for many companies is the most important profit-generating asset.

Up to this point we have seen how accounting information is used in the planning process. Once planning has been completed and decisions have been made, however, accounting information is equally important in controlling operations and ensuring that plan results are realized.

Although managers need a certain amount of information to make control decisions, unnecessary information causes confusion. The more irrelevant information they are provided with, the more information they must sort through to find the facts they need. This factor has become even more important with the advent of the computer and the creation of what some call "information overload."

In the past, managers were often faulted for making poor decisions because they did not have enough information. Now, with the computer, it may well be that the opposite is true.

RESPONSIBILITY ACCOUNTING

Control is the action that a business person takes to ensure that actual results correspond to planned results. To control a business, managers need information detailing the results of specific activities. If a company offers several product lines in many sales regions, managers must know how much each product is contributing to the profitability of each regional operation. Such information is necessary to determine where special action is needed. To provide managers with this type of information, managerial accountants prepare segment reports, or detailed reports on particular aspects of a business.

In a small organization, one person can follow operations and make almost all important decisions. As a company grows and operations become more complex, however, some division of responsibility is needed. As a result, decision-making managers delegate authority to subordinates, who assume responsibility for the financial results of their decisions.

There are three major patterns in which these managerial responsibilities are delegated:
1. Business function
2. Product line
3. Geographic region

Many companies are organized primarily by business function. In such a situation a manager may be responsible for one of the four major business functions:
1. Production
2. Marketing
3. Finance
4. Human Resources

Larger companies often organize operations by product line. In this type of organization a single manager is responsible for the production, marketing, finance, and human resources involved in a specific product line. For instance, this type of organization is appropriate for a computer company selling both large computers and microcomputers.

Another common organizational structure is a geographic organization. It allows one manager to make almost all functional decisions for a geographic region. In a nation as large as the United States a company's operations are separated into regions such as Southeast, Midwest, Northeast, and West. Smaller countries such as England or France might fall into a single region.

FINANCIAL RESPONSIBILITY CENTERS AND THEIR ACCOUNTING NEEDS

What should business people be responsible for?

Of course, not all managers have the same type of financial responsibility. Some control only expenses; others control revenues; some managers control both. In order to make good decisions, however, managers need reliable, timely, and relevant information. Organizational units are generally considered centers of financial responsibility, and each unit has its own accounting needs. Financial responsibility falls into four categories:

- Expense center
- Revenue center
- Profit center
- Investment center

An expense center manager must ensure that assigned tasks are completed within the limits allowed by budgets or standard costs of the type discussed in earlier chapters. The responsibility accounting system should supply managers with information needed to schedule workers efficiently, to avoid wasting materials, supplies and energy, and to use equipment productively. Expense centers are sometimes called cost centers.

The manager of a revenue center is responsible for selling budgeted quantities of products or services at budgeted prices (gross income). A sales representative selling bread to grocery stores, a sales manager distributing automobiles to dealers in specific geographic areas, and the manager of a furniture department in a large department store are all managers of revenue centers.

The manager of a profit center is responsible for controlling both expenses and revenues to achieve a budgeted profit (net income). The manager of a new car department of a local automobile dealer is usually a manager of a profit center. He or she controls profits by purchasing the right cars, setting sales commissions to motivate sales representatives, and using advertising and other expenditures to generate sales.

Finally, the manager of an investment center is responsible for controlling expenses, revenues, and investments to achieve a budgeted return on an investment (ROI). Such managers have the broadest responsibility. A chief executive officer has such responsibility, as do managers of divisions in some large organizations. In financial terms, the return on investment (ROI) is the ratio of the profit earned by an investment center to the investment attributable to that center.

ASSIGNING COSTS TO ORGANIZATIONAL SEGMENTS

In order to properly control a subdivision of a company, relevant costs must be assigned to that activity, often called a segment. Product lines, sales territories, customer groupings, divisions, and manufacturing operations are all examples of segments. Each of these segments contributes separately to a company's objectives and must be evaluated on its own merits. But it is important that a business person be evaluated only on matters over which he or she has control.

As we saw earlier, a company's contribution to profit is the difference between sales revenue and variable costs. The contribution margin for a segment is also the difference between sales revenues and these costs. But calculating a segment's contribution margin involves more than collecting sales data and variable costs for each segment. The accountant must also separate many of the company's expenses into two categories—direct costs and common costs—and assign them to segments.

Earlier we defined a direct cost as a cost physically traceable to a product or service. In that sense direct material and direct labor costs are such costs for a particular product. A direct cost to an organizational segment, however, is a cost that can be physically traced to that segment. For example, in an organization segmented by product lines, direct materials and direct labor costs are considered direct costs to a product line. Some companies have separate manufacturing plants for each product line. In that case all the manufacturing costs incurred in a plant are assigned directly to the plant and to the product line.

A common cost is one that benefits more than one product or service or organization segment at the same time. It is the opposite of a direct cost, which benefits only one product, service, or organizational segment. If an organization is segmented by product line, but more than one product is produced in a manufacturing plant, then depreciation on that plant is a common cost.

Another example would be the salary of a company president. If the cost objective is the entire company, the president's salary is a direct cost. But if the cost objective is one product line or sales territory among many in the company, then the president's salary is a common cost.

The concepts we are talking about here are similar to the variable cost ideas discussed earlier. Thus, in some cases costs are closely tied to an activity or a segment of a company or product, whereas at other times they are not. The skill of managerial accounting lies in associating those costs that are not so closely tied into a product or an activity with those products or activities in a way that enables the company's managers to make some meaningful conclusions. As a result, for control purposes there are product line reports, territory reports, reports by types of customers that the business has, all of which enable people responsible for those products, territories, or customers to have a better feel for what costs are involved in serving that purpose.

It is therefore important that managerial accounting reports should be custom designed to the needs of managers. Segment reports fulfill that aim by clearly identifying the revenues and cost within a manager's control.

ASSIGNING COSTS TO INVENTORY: DIRECT COSTING VS. ABSORPTION COSTING

When business managers design an accounting system, they must choose a method for inventory evaluation. For external reporting, full-absorption costing is required, as we saw in the chapter on financial accounting. Full-absorption costing combines variable and fixed manufacturing costs in the product cost. However, this often creates manufacturing cost information that is not appropriate for preparing income statements using the contribution margin format. Because of this, managerial accountants prefer direct costing, which does not combine variable and fixed manufacturing cost and is consistent with the contribution margin format.

When absorption costing is used, direct materials, direct labor, and manufacturing overhead costs (both fixed and variable) are absorbed into the value of inventory. This method must be used in external financial reports such as cost of goods manufactured and sold and in the costing of inventory on the balance sheet. The rationale behind this requirement is that proper matching of revenues and expenses requires that all expenses related to the revenues must be reported in the same period as the revenues.

When the second method (called direct costing) is used, only direct materials, direct labor, and variable manufacturing overheads are utilized in the value of inventory. Fixed manufacturing overhead costs are excluded from this computation and are instead treated as period expenses, much like the fixed selling and administrative costs discussed in Chapter 6. The rationale behind this treatment of fixed manufacturing costs is that these costs will be incurred regardless of how many units are produced. Hence they represent the cost of providing productive capacity for the period. Therefore, these total costs should be expensed in the period in which they provide capacity, with no portion assigned to inventory. The reason is that the people responsible for producing the product have no control over these costs. Consequently their performance should not be measured on the basis of costs incurred in the period over which they have no control.

The following example illustrates both these points. Michelle Corporation produces a single product. Financial data on the company's 1989 operations is as follows:

MICHELLE CORPORATION

Number of units expected to be sold		3,800
Number of units expected to be produced		4,000
Beginning inventory, finished units		0
Estimated ending inventory, finished units		200
Selling price per unit		$19,000
Variable costs per unit		
Direct materials	$1.00	
Direct labor	4.00	
Variable manufacturing overhead	2.00	
Variable selling and administrative	1.50	$ 8.50
Fixed costs for 1989		
Manufacturing overhead		$12,000
Selling and administrative		20,000

Depending on the method used to cost Michelle's inventory, the value per unit will be $10 or $7 as shown below:

ABSORPTION COSTING

Direct materials	$ 1.00
Direct labor	4.00
Variable manufacturing overhead	2.00
Fixed manufacturing overhead	
$12,000 per year ÷ 4,000 units produced	3.00
Total inventory costs	$10.00

DIRECT COSTING

Direct materials	$ 1.00
Direct labor	4.00
Variable manufacturing overhead	2.00
Total inventory cost	$ 7.00

Notice that inventory costs are lower under direct costing because fixed overhead is excluded from the calculation. On the other hand, the costs involved in the direct cost method are those that a manager would be held responsible for. In fact, it is through the use of costs of this type that a manager's performance can be measured. In situations where performance measurement is important for operating people, the direct costing approach would be utilized.

CHAPTER PERSPECTIVE

In this chapter we have begun the process of utilizing managerial accounting to measure the performance of business managers and employees. We have seen how responsibilities for various business activities can be assigned on a functional basis, a product line basis, or a geographic basis. We have also seen that costs can be related to these various subsections of the business so that performance of the people responsible for their conduct can be measured. Finally, we have had an opportunity of seeing how inventory costs are attributed to the various types of products being manufactured so that the performance of people involved in the production side of a company can be measured.

Standard Costs for Material and Labor

INTRODUCTION AND MAIN POINTS

In this chapter we will expand your knowledge of setting criteria for your business to meet in order to make certain that you're performing at the level you expect and meet the targets you are setting for your business. In Chapter 15 we talked about measuring responsibility of managers in various ways, namely, by the business functions in which they're active, by the production areas in which they're involved, and by the geographic areas for which they're responsible. In all of these ways of measuring responsibility there are standards that can be set at the beginning of a period so that you'll be able to measure performance against expectations on a moving forward basis.

Consequently, in this chapter we'll concentrate on how to set standard costs for the materials the firm uses and the labor it employs during the operating cycle.

After studying the material in this chapter:

━ You will understand what constitutes the standards for materials and labor in your business.

━ You will be able to appreciate the portion of the standard that is impacted by changes in the quantities of material and labor you use.

━ You will appreciate the extent to which changes in prices will impact your performance.

━ You will know how to determine variances from the materials and labor standards that a business will incur.

━ You will have an understanding of how to analyze these variances so that you can take action to correct any changes from the standards set at the beginning of the period.

Standards of one type or another are used to evaluate many activities. Universities set minimum grade-point standards for graduating students and for awarding honors. Designers of golf courses set an average course score, or par, against which players may compare their own scores.

Standards also determine the price you pay for some services. Automotive shops charge for repairs based on a standard time allowed for the work. For example, the standard time allowed for a tune-up might be one hour. That same standard can be used to evaluate the mechanics' efficiency for the actual time they take to perform a job. Standards are used for business planning and control as well. Manufacturing companies use standards to predict the per-unit manufacturing costs of products before they are produced. Such information monitors costs as products move through production.

In technical terms a standard cost per unit is a predetermined cost consisting of two components:

1. A cost component based on a *quantity* of one standard per unit of finished product. The quantity standard is expressed in terms of some measure of input, such as number of pounds, gallons, or direct labor hours for one unit of output.

2. A cost component based on a *price* standard for each measure of input. The price standard is expressed in monetary terms per measure of input, such as dollars per pound, per gallon, or per direct labor hour of input.

Standard cost, a very powerful cost control element, is calculated by multiplying the quantity standard for each unit by the price standard for that unit (i.e., total standard cost equals quantity standard × price standard).

From a cost accounting perspective, standard costs simplify the process of assigning inventory a value so that cost of goods sold can be determined. From a managerial accounting perspective, standard costs facilitate the planning and control of operations, since they are used as measures in preparing budgets (the planning function) and in measuring performance (the control function).

To prepare a budget, a manager must find the quantities needed of each direct material and type of direct labor in order to produce the planned level of output. Next, the cost is determined by multiplying each standard input by its price standard. Let's assume that a company plans to produce a thousand units of product. Since their standards specify that two pounds of a direct material are needed for each finished unit, the standard input quantity for a 1,000-unit end product would be 2,000 pounds. Finally, assume the standard price is $4.00 per pound of the direct material; the expected cost would then be $8,000.

With regard to measuring performance, many variables affect the costs of producing a product. Managers are expected to continue to control these variables to the extent that their authority permits. To know whether their costs are within bounds, managers need a yardstick for comparing actual costs. Standard costs serve this purpose because they represent the expected cost of producing one unit of the product. Thus, by comparing actual costs against standard costs, a manager can see the difference between actual and planned expenditures, called a variance.

Any significant variance from standard costs indicates that operations are not proceeding as planned and that corrective action might be needed.

DIRECT MATERIALS VARIANCES

Like all standard costs, those for direct materials consist of two components: a quantity standard and a price standard. The *quantity standard* represents the amount of input that goes into producing one unit of output. The *price standard* is the price management expects to pay for a unit of input, again in this case a direct material.

Once quantity and price standards are established, they can be used to evaluate actual costs by calculating variances. Variances from direct material standards stem from two sources:

1. Differences between the actual quantity of materials used and standard quantities allowed for a given period's actual output
2. Differences between the actual price paid for direct materials and standard prices

An easier way to understand this would be through an example. Assume that the Schiff Company has set the following standards for one of its products:

Standard price per pound of direct material is $4.00.

Standard quantity of direct materials per unit of product is two.

Standard cost of direct materials is $8.00 per unit.

If the company produces 3,000 units in the first quarter, standard quantity of direct material allowed would be 6,000 pounds. (i.e., 2 pounds standard × 3,000 units).

The second step is to find the difference between the actual quantity of direct materials used and the standard quantity of the direct materials allowed. Multiplying this difference by the standard price per unit of direct materials yields the quantity variance in dollars.

The standard price per unit of direct materials is the price a company expects to pay per unit of direct material. When calculating the quantity variance, the standard price is used instead of the actual price to ensure measurement consistency over the year. The standard price usually remains constant over a year, while actual prices may fluctuate. By using a standard price in the calculation, differences in quantity variance reflect changes in efficiency by change in price. In the case of the Schiff Company, assume that 6,100 pounds of materials were used. The dollar value of the quantity variance is 6,100 pounds minus 6,000 pounds times $4.00, or $400 of unfavorable variance; see Figure 16-1.

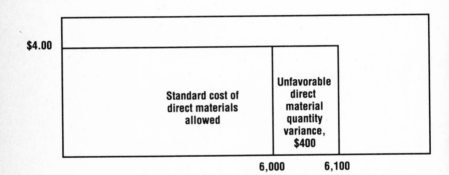

FIG. 16-1 *Graphic illustration of direct materials quantity variance for the company*

The direct material price variance is the difference between the actual price per unit of direct material and a standard price multiplied by the actual quantity of materials purchased. This calculation is used to determine the total amount of money saved (or expended) because of the price differences. The computation for a price variance equals the actual price per unit less the standard price per unit times the actual quantity of the direct materials purchased. This is illustrated in Figure 16-2.

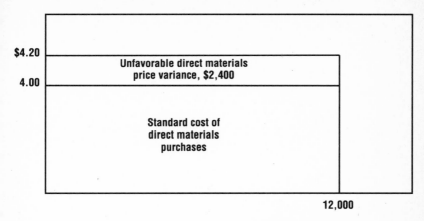

FIG. 16-2 *Graphic illustration of direct materials price variance for the Thompson Company*

DIRECT LABOR VARIANCES

There are similar techniques in the managerial accounting area for computing labor cost variances. In this case the quantity standard would be the amount of direct labor required for a unit of output. In many companies quantity standards are established by engineering analysis.

The direct labor price standard is actually a labor rate standard. It represents the labor rate a company expects to pay for one hour of labor category for the year. The human resources department of a company is usually consulted in this area, as they are most familiar with the local labor market.

As you can see from the graph in Figure 16-3, the standard labor rate is $20.00 per hour while the actual average labor rate was $19.50. The standard quantity of direct labor hours allowed was 6,000 hours, but the actual quantity was only 5,800 hours.

177

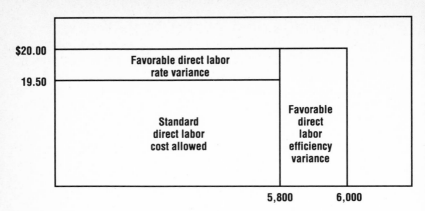

FIG. 16-3 *Graphic illustration of direct labor efficiency and rate variances*

The results of this are summarized as follows:

THOMPSON COMPANY
COMPUTATION OF DIRECT LABOR VARIANCES

Actual Direct Labor Hours Used × Actual Rate	*Actual Direct Labor Hours Used × Standard Rate*	*Standard Direct Labor Hours Allowed × Standard Rate*
5,800 hours	5,800 hours	6,000 hours
× $ 19.50 per hour	× $ 20.00 per hour	× $ 20.00 per hour
$113,100	$116,000	$120,000
Rate Variance: $2,900 (favorable)	Efficiency Variance: $4,000 (favorable)	Total Direct Labor Variance: $6,900 (favorable)

INVESTIGATING VARIANCES

Direct materials and direct labor variances represent the difference between an expected cost and an actual cost. The variance is significant and signals that one of two actions should be taken.

1. The causes of variances must be determined and corrected so that standard costs can be achieved.

2. The standards should be revised as they no longer are attainable.

How large should a variance be before it is investigated? To investigate a variance and take corrective action involves cost to an organization. That cost should be only incurred when there is a reasonable chance that benefits will exceed cost. Variances representing minor deviations from budgeted amounts caused only by random fluctuations in business operations should not be investigated.

Should only unfavorable variances be investigated? Definitely not. For one thing, investigating favorable variances might reveal improved operating procedures applicable to other parts of the organization. The favorable variance might also suggest that a standard cost should be changed.

Many sophisticated techniques for analyzing variances have been developed by managerial accountants. It should be remembered that computing variances is not the end result of the exercise. Rather, an educated analysis of the variances is the key to the use of the accounting information generated by the managerial accounting. A trained eye, the knowledge of the business, and a feeling for the numbers is needed to make a worthwhile variance analysis. Many managers develop a rule of thumb based on their managerial experience in order to determine what variances need to be investigated.

For people less knowledgeable about the business, the basic concept of statistical quality control has been developed. This method assumes that a business activity has some stable pattern of variability when measurements of a repetitive process are taken (e.g., producing golf balls). As long as the measurements are within that pattern, the process is considered to be in the state of statistical control. As shown in Figure 16-4, a measurement outside of the pattern is a signal that the process is out of control and should be investigated.

CHAPTER PERSPECTIVE

In this chapter you have had exposure to an important concept in business management—variance analysis. What this means is you now have an idea of how to compute a difference between the standards set for the amount of material to use in making a product, the number of labor hours needed to produce it, the prices the firm pays for those inputs, and how those items differ from the standards you set at the beginning of the period. Variance analysis is part of the homework you can do to determine why expectations are not being met, meeting either on the plus side or the minus side. This discussion will get a little more complex in the next chapter, where we will look at a way of computing the standards so as to keep an ongoing measurement of actual activity versus budgeted activity through the medium of flexible budgeting.

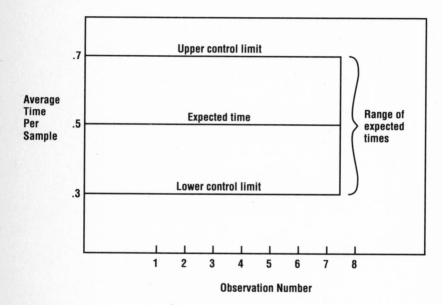

FIG. 16-4 *Statistical control chart*

Flexible Budgets and Overhead Costs

CHAPTER 17

INTRODUCTION AND MAIN POINTS

In this chapter you will build on the knowledge you received in Chapter 16 dealing with standard cost by investigating the idea of flexible budgeting. Flexible budgeting essentially means that, if you set a budget at the beginning of the year and do not change it as circumstances altered during the year, you are going to have a rigid ruler for measuring your performance all during the year. You will see that, in the area involving overhead costs, such an approach tends not to give the business person the ability to make mid course corrections as circumstances change during the year. For this reason this chapter will examine the way flexible budgets can be set for overhead costs to give you a better measurement standard.

After studying the material in this chapter:

■ You will understand the difference between static and flexible budgets as a tool for conducting business.

■ You will know how to apply flexible budgeting to manufacturing overhead costs.

■ You will see how overhead cost standards are set.

■ You will be able to determine how overhead variances are computed from a cost as well as a volume standpoint in a manner analogous to the variances we saw in Chapter 16.

■ You will have an idea of how flexible budgeting is used for nonmanufacturing activities.

The reader should note that this chapter contains rather complicated material dealing with the subject of overhead standards and variances related to those standards. It may be beyond the needs the reader has for basic understanding of the subject in his or her particular business or divisional activity in a company. Illustrations have been used liberally to try and make the necessary points clearly and simply. It should be noted at this point, however, that after this level of complication the average business person would seek the expertise of accountants who deal on a continuous basis with the subject of manufacturing standards and variance analysis.

Flexible budgets are especially useful for evaluating the performance of a department manager. (The term "flexible budget" means a budget that is adjusted during the course of the business cycle in recognition of the fact that levels of business activity have changed during the period, and budgets should be recomputed to give recognition to that change.) Before flexible budgets, firms used to use budgets based on the estimated level of production to cost products and to evaluate manager's performance. Those budgets were called static budgets and were not revised even if the actual production level differed from the estimated level. Since production estimates were made for a year in advance, they rarely matched actual volume. They often were more theoretical than practical.

Production level is significant because variable overhead costs change if production changes. For example, the total cost of electricity increases with the number of machine-hours. A flexible overhead budget automatically increases the cost allowed for electricity when machine-hours increase. A static budget would not. It would provide one amount for electricity regardless of the production level.

As a result, static budgets are rarely used for evaluating performance. On the other hand, a flexible budget tells managers how much manufacturing overhead should have been incurred at the level of production that did actually occur. Any difference between the actual and flexible budgeted overhead reflect potential cost-control problems that warrant investigation.

It is not the purpose of this book to delve into details of the computation of flexible budgets. However, these budgets are such an important measurement tool that a bit more information might be warranted at this point, in order to give you a feeling for how to use a flexible budget in your firm's business activities.

SELECTING AN ACTIVITY BASE

To develop a flexible overhead budget the accountant must first select a suitable measure of production activity. This is called the *activity base*. The item is usually not finished units but direct labor-hours, machine-hours, or some similar base. Units of product are generally not used because overhead costs usually benefit several products. For example, if several different products are produced on a machine, the cost of maintaining the machine benefits all the products. However, the products may be so different from each other that one product takes considerably more machine time than the others. To measure the machine's total production, one needs an activity measure common to all products produced on it—such as machine-hours. The activity base that one selects therefore has to be the one that best relates manufacturing overhead to production volume. It is the one that best measures how manufacturing overhead costs vary with that production volume.

Let us start with an example using the basic figures shown in the Jordan Corporation's flexible budget.

JORDAN CORPORATION
FLEXIBLE BUDGET FOR 5,000 MACHINE-HOURS
FOR THE MONTH OF JUNE, 1989

Estimated machine-hours

3,000 large disks × 1.0 standard machine-hours	= 3,000
4,000 small disks × 0.5 standard machine-hours	= 2,000
Total planned machine-hours	5,000

	Fixed Costs	Variable Costs	Total Costs for 5,000* Machine-Hours
Controllable costs			
Indirect labor		$1.50	$ 7,500
Cutting tools		0.05	2,500
Lubricants		0.20	1,000
Power	$ 600	0.30	2,100
Allocated costs			
Maintenance	3,000	0.05	5,500
Noncontrollable costs			
Supervision	6,000		6,000
Depreciation	25,400		25,400
Total costs	$35,000	$3.00	$50,000

*Because this budget is for a machining department, machine-hours are used to measure production activity. Were the budget for an assembly department, it could be expressed in direct labor-hours.

MANUFACTURING OVERHEAD STANDARDS

Once the appropriate activity base is identified, a standard applied manufacturing overhead cost is useful for product costing. As contrasted to direct materials and direct labor standards (discussed in Chapter 16), a manufacturing overhead standard is not useful for planning and control.

This is because a manufacturing overhead standard treats fixed overhead costs as variable. For that reason more complicated flexible budgets have to be used for planning and control of overhead costs. A predetermined overhead rate is calculated by dividing the estimated manufacturing overhead cost for the year by the estimated annual production volume. Such a predetermined overhead rate base on machine-hours is based as follows:

Predetermined overhead rate based on machine-hours *equals* Estimated total annual overhead *divided by* Estimated annual machine-hours.

This can best be understood by following the calculations in Table 17-1.

Table 17-1

Calculating the Predetermined Overhead Rate

Accountants at Jordan Corporation have gathered the following information for the machining department:

Estimated variable overhead rate	$3.00 per machine-hour
Estimated fixed overhead costs	$420,000 per year
Estimated production volume	60,000 machine-hours per year

To calculate a predetermined overhead rate, the accountant estimates the total overhead cost for the year, calculated by using the flexible budget formula:

Total cost = fixed costs per year
+ (variable costs per activity measure × production volume)

Estimated annual overhead costs = $420,000 + ($3.00 × 60,000 machine-hours)
= $600,000

Finally, the predetermined overhead rate is figured:

$$\text{Predetermined overhead rate} = \frac{\text{estimated annual overhead costs}}{\text{estimated annual machine-hours}}$$

$$= \frac{\$600,000}{60,000 \text{ machine-hours}}$$

$$= \$10 \text{ per machine-hour}$$

For calculating volume variances, it is useful to break the predetermined overhead rate into its fixed and variable components as follows:

$$\frac{\text{estimated annual fixed overhead}}{\text{estimated annual machine-hours}} + \frac{\text{estimated annual variable overhead}}{\text{estimated annual machine-hours}}$$

$$\frac{\$420,000}{60,000 \text{ machine-hours}} + \frac{\$180,000}{60,000 \text{ machine-hours}} = \frac{\$600,000}{60,000 \text{ machine-hours}}$$

$$= \$7.00 \text{ per machine-hour} + \$3.00 \text{ per machine-hour} = \$10.00 \text{ per machine-hour}$$

Calculating the Standard Applied Manufacturing Overhead Cost Per Unit

By using the combined predetermined overhead rate as computed above and standard activity measure per unit, you can calculate the standard applied manufacturing overhead cost per unit. The formula is as follows:

Standard applied manufacturing overhead cost per unit *equals* Predetermined overhead rate *multiplied by* Planned amount of activity measure per unit of output.

For Jordan Corporation products, the computation is as follows:

Standard applied manufacturing overhead = $10 per machine-hour × 1 machine-hour

Costs, large disk = $10 per unit

Standard applied manufacturing overhead = $10 per machine-hour × 0.5 machine-hour

Costs, small disk = $5 per unit

Manufacturing Overhead Variances

With these standards computed, actual overhead cost may vary from standard overhead costs for several reasons. Variances related to specific reasons can be calculated. The budget variance represents that part of the total overhead variance that can be attributed to the difference between the actual overhead cost and estimated overhead cost. The volume variance represents that part of total overhead variance that can be attributed to the difference between the actual production volume and the average production volume on which the predetermined overhead rate is based. In this way it is possible to identify the reasons why the variances take place in order to determine where corrective action has to be taken.

In order to give you some perspective on what the elements are, the diagram in Figure 17-1 sets forth the various types of manufacturing overhead variances.

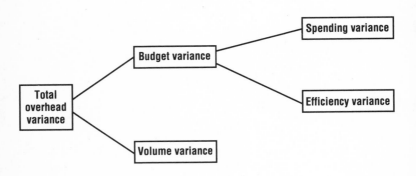

FIG. 17-1

BUDGET VARIANCE

The budget variance portion is the difference between actual manufacturing overhead cost and budgeted cost based on the standard quantity of machine-hours allowed for the actual number of units produced. It indicates the amount of variable manufacturing overhead cost saved or overspent because of the efficient or inefficient use of machine time.

Budget variance *equals* Actual manufacturing overhead cost *minus* Flexible budget overhead cost for standard quantity of machine-hours allowed for the number of units produced.

If we continue with the Jordan Corporation example, the first step in calculating the budget variance is to find the standard quantity of machine-hours allowed for the actual production level. Using standard machine-hours per unit from page 000, you then get a standard quantity of machine-hours allowed of 3,000 for the large disk and 1,900 for the small disk—a total of 4,900:

Standard quantity of machine-hours allowed	=	Standard quantity of machine-hours per unit	×	Number of units produced

Large disk:	3,000	=	1 × 3,000	
Small disk:	1,900	=	0.5 × 3,800	
Total	4,900			

In this example let us say the estimated time for the month of June was reported to be 5,000 hours. This number is the estimated average monthly standard machine-hours, calculated by dividing the estimated annual output of 60,000 standard machine-hours by 12. We note from this situation that budgeted fixed costs are $35,000 per month and variable costs are $3.00 per machine-hour. Using these costs, we can calculate flexible budget overhead costs for 4,900 machine-hours as follows:

Fixed costs ($35,000) *plus* Variable costs ($3.00 × 4,900 = $14,700) *equals* $49,700.

Let us now assume that actual manufacturing overhead costs total $49,854. Thus the budget variance is $49,854 minus $49,700 = $154 unfavorable variance. This is set forth in the accompanying Jordan Corporation budget variance report.

JORDAN CORPORATION
BUDGET VARIANCE REPORT: MACHINING DEPARTMENT
FOR THE MONTH OF JUNE, 1989

Cost Items	Actual Overhead Costs	Flexible Budget Overhead Costs for 4,900 Standard Machine-Hours	Budget Variances
A. Controllable			
Indirect labor	$ 7,595	$ 7,350(1)	$245 (unfavorable)
Cutting tools	2,500	2,450(2)	50 (unfavorable)
Lubricants	1,029	980(3)	49 (unfavorable)
Power	1,825	2,070(4)	245 (favorable)
B. Allocated			
Maintenance	5,255	5,450(5)	195 (favorable)
C. Noncontrollable			
Supervision	6,250	6,000	250 (unfavorable)
Depreciation	25,400	25,400	0
Total	$49,854	$49,700	$154 (unfavorable)

FOOTNOTES

(1) *$1.50 per machine-hour × 4,900 standard machine-hours*

(2) *$.50 per machine-hour × 4,900 standard machine-hours*

(3) *$.20 per machine-hour × 4,900 standard machine-hours*

(4) *$600 + $.30 per machine-hour × 4,900 standard machine-hours*

(5) *$3,000 + $.50 per machine-hour × 4,900 standard machine-hours*

A graphic way of displaying this analysis is set forth in Figure 17-2.

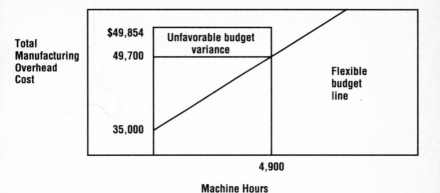

FIG. 17-2 *Jordan Corporation: Graphic analysis of a manufacturing overhead budget variance*

This budget variance can be further refined by being subdivided into a *spending* variance and an *efficiency* variance.

SPENDING VARIANCE

The spending variance is the difference between actual overhead costs and budgeted overhead costs for the actual activity during the period. This variance is based on one assumption. The best measure of how money should have been spent on manufacturing overhead is computed by using the actual, not the standard, number of machine-hours or direct labor-hours.

The spending variance is calculated as follows:

Spending variance *equals* Total actual manufacturing overhead cost *minus* Flexible budget overhead cost for actual quantity of machine-hours used.

The only difference between this formula and the one for the budget variance is the use of actual machine-hours rather than standard machine-hours. Flexible budget overhead costs for the actual quantity of machine-hours used can be found by using the information in the following report:

JORDAN CORPORATION
FLEXIBLE BUDGET FOR 5,000 MACHINE-HOURS
FOR THE MONTH OF JUNE, 1989

Estimated machine-hours

3,000 large disks × 1.0 standard machine-hours	= 3,000
4,000 small disks × 0.5 standard machine-hours	= 2,000
Total planned machine-hours	5,000

	Actual Costs	Variable Costs	Total Costs for 5,000* Machine-Hours
Controllable costs			
Indirect labor		$1.50	$ 7,500
Cutting tools		0.50	2,500
Lubricants		0.20	1,000
Power	600	0.30	2,100
Allocated costs			
Maintenance	3,000	0.05	5,500
Noncontrollable costs			
Supervision	6,000		6,000
Depreciation	25,400		25,400
Total	$35,000	$3.00	$50,000

Because the budget is for a machining department, machine-hours are used to measure production activity. Were the budget for an assembly department, it would be expressed in direct labor-hours.

Jordan budgeted fixed overhead costs are 35,000 per month; its variable cost, $3.00 per machine-hour. Let's assume that 5,100 actual machine-hours were used. Therefore flexible budget costs for actual machine-hours are fixed $35,000 and variable ($3.00 × 5,100) = $15,300 for a total of $50,300.

The details of this favorable variance can be seen in the following report:

JORDAN CORPORATION
BUDGET VARIANCE REPORT: MACHINING DEPARTMENT
FOR THE MONTH OF JUNE, 1989

Cost Items	Actual Overhead Costs	Flexible Budget Overhead Costs for 5,100 Standard Machine-Hours	Budget Variances
A. Controllable			
Indirect labor . . .	$ 7,595	$ 7,650(1)	$ 55 (favorable)
Cutting tools . . .	2,500	2,550(2)	50 (favorable)
Lubricants	1,029	1,020(3)	9 (unfavorable)
Power	1,825	2,130(4)	305 (favorable)
B. Allocated			
Maintenance . . .	5,255	5,550(5)	295 (unfavorable)
C. Noncontrollable			
Supervision	6,250	6,000	250 (unfavorable)
Depreciation . . .	25,400	25,400	0
Total	$49,854	$50,300	$446 (favorable)

FOOTNOTES
(1) *$1.50 per machine-hour × 5,100 actual machine-hours*
(2) *$.50 per machine-hour × 5,100 actual machine-hours*
(3) *$.20 per machine-hour × 5,100 actual machine-hours*
(4) *$600 + $.30 per machine-hour × 5,100 actual machine-hours*
(5) *$3,000 + $.50 per machine-hour × 5,100 actual machine-hours*

EFFICIENCY VARIANCE
The other part of the budget variance is called the efficiency variance. This is the difference between the flexible budget overhead cost for actual machine-hours used and flexible budget overhead cost for the standard quantity of machine-hours allowed.

The formula for the efficiency variance is as follows:

Efficiency variance *equals* Flexible budget overhead cost for actual quantity of machine-hours used *minus* Flexible overhead budget cost for the standard quantity of machine-hours allowed.

Continuing the Jordan Corporation example, both cost figures needed to calculate their efficiency variance have been computed. Flexible budget overhead cost for 5,100 actual machine-hours was found when the spending variance was calculated—$50,300. Flexible budget overhead costs for 4,900 standard machine-hours were found when calculating the budget variance earlier—$49,700.

The difference between these two figures gives us the efficiency variance of $600 unfavorable. The variance is unfavorable because the number of actual machine-hours is greater than the standard number of machine-hours allowed.

A graphic display of the combination of spending and efficiency variance is set forth below:

JORDAN CORPORATION
SPENDING AND EFFICIENCY VARIANCE:
MACHINING DEPARTMENT
FOR THE MONTH OF JUNE, 1989

Cost Item	(a) Actual Overhead Costs	(b) Flexible Budget Overhead Costs for 5,100 Actual Machine-Hours	(c) Flexible Budget Overhead Costs for 4,900 Standard Machine-Hours	(a) − (b) Spending Variance	(b) − (c) Efficiency Variance
A. Controllable					
Indirect labor	$ 7,595	$ 7,650	$ 7,350	$ 55(F)	
Cutting tools	2,500	2,550	2,450	50(F)	
Lubricants . . .	1,029	1,020	980	9(U)	
Power	1,825	2,130	2,070	305(F)	
B. Allocated					
Maintenance	5,255	5,550	5,450	295(F)	
C. Noncontrollable					
Supervision . .	6,250	6,000	6,000	250(U)	
Depreciation . .	25,400	25,400	25,400	0	
Total	$49,854	$50,300	$49,700	$446(F)	$600(U)

FOOTNOTES

(F) *Favorable*

(U) *Unfavorable*

VOLUME VARIANCE

The volume variance is a measure of the difference between the actual production volume and the average monthly production volume on which the predetermined overhead rate is based. It can be determined by the difference between the applied overhead and flexible budget overhead for the actual number of units produced. Standard machine-hours should be used to calculate both figures. This is an important point. When applied overhead was calculated for job order costing, actual hours, not standard hours, were used in determining the amount of overhead cost applied to units produced. But in standard costing you have to use standard hours because overhead costs, unlike direct materials and direct labor costs, are applied on the basis of what is allowed for each unit produced using the predetermined overhead rate per unit.

The volume variance is calculated as follows:

> Volume variance *equals* Flexible budget overhead costs for the standard quantity of machine-hours allowed for the number of units produced, *minus* Applied manufacturing overhead costs for the standard quantity of machine-hours allowed for the number of units produced.

Continuing our Jordan Corporation example, let's assume they had 4,900 standard machine-hours allowed and flexible budget overhead costs for those standard machine-hours were $49,700.

Applied overhead for those standard machine-hours is calculated using Jordan Corporation's total predetermined overhead rate of $10.00 per machine-hour. That is 4,900 × $10.00 per machine-hour = 49,000.

Substituting these two total figures in the formula above, $49,700 − 49,000 = $700 unfavorable variance.

Another way of calculating the volume variance would be to multiply the fixed overhead rate by the difference between the estimated average monthly standard quantity of machine-hours allowed and the standard quantity of machine-hours allowed for the number of units actually produced.

For the Jordan Corporation the computation is $7.00 × (5,000 − 4,900) = $700 unfavorable variance.

The thing to keep in mind is that the volume variance is a quantity measure, not a cost measure. It indicates whether actual production volume was above or below the estimated average monthly production volume. Jordan Corporation's production allowed only 4,900 standard machine-hours as opposed to the monthly average of 5,000 machine-hours. The difference of 100 machine-hours caused the $700 unfavorable volume variance.

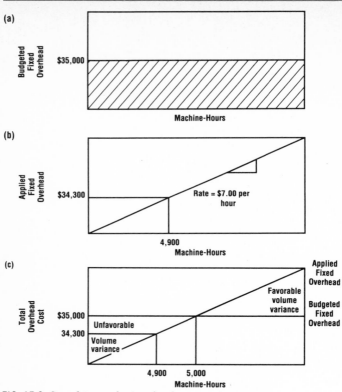

FIG. 17-3 *Graphic analysis of volume variance*

Had Jordan produced at a level of more than 5,000 hours, its volume variance would have been favorable (see the cross-hatched area in the exhibits above).

To summarize, the total manufacturing overhead variance is the difference between actual manufacturing costs and applied overhead costs. When a standard cost system is used, overhead costs are applied on the basis of total standard hours allowed for the number of units produced.

For Jordan Corporation the total overhead variance is $49,854 minus $49,000 ($10.00 × 4,900) = $854 underapplied. The overhead variance is considered underapplied because actual overhead costs are more than applied overhead costs.

The table summarizes the computation of manufacturing overhead variances. Column 1 shows the actual manufacturing

JORDAN CORPORATION

MANUFACTURING OVERHEAD VARIANCES: MACHINING DEPARTMENT

FOR THE MONTH OF JUNE, 1989

Cost Behavior Classification	(1) Actual Overhead Costs	(2) Flexible Budget Overhead Costs for 5,100 Actual Machine-Hours	(3) Flexible Budget Overhead Costs for 4,900 Standard Machine-Hours	(4) Applied Manufacturing Overhead for 4,900 Standard Machine-Hours
Variable		$15,300(1)	$14,700(1)	$14,700
Fixed		35,000(1)	35,00(1)	34,300
Total	$49,854(1)	$50,300	$49,700	$49,000

$446 Favorable spending variance

$154 Unfavorable budget variance

$600 Unfavorable efficiency variance

$700 Unfavorable volume variance

$854 Total manufacturing overhead variance (underapplied)

overhead costs and column 2 shows flexible budget overhead costs for the actual number of machine-hours used. The difference between columns 1 and 2 is the spending variance. For Jordan Corporation this variance is a favorable $446.

Column 3 shows flexible overhead costs for standard machine-hours allowed for the units produced. The difference between columns 2 and 3 is the efficiency variance for Jordan Corporation. This variance is an unfavorable $600. (The difference between columns 1 and 3 is the overall budget variance, which is the sum of the spending and the efficiency variances.)

Finally, column 4 shows the applied manufacturing overhead costs for the standard machine-hours allowed. The difference between columns 3 and 4 is the volume variance, here an unfavorable $700. The difference between columns 1 and 4 is the total manufacturing overhead variance, which is the sum of the budget and volume variances.

CAUSES OF MANUFACTURING OVERHEAD VARIANCES

Before managers can investigate overhead variances and take appropriate action, they must understand the causes of these variances. The causes differ, depending on whether the cost involved is controllable, allocated, or noncontrollable. If a cost is noncontrollable, then it should not be charged to the person whose performance is being measured. Consequently, these costs have to be placed at the feet of people who contracted for them.

On the other hand, if a cost is controllable or allocated, then a manager can be held responsible for those costs.

It must be recalled that controllable costs are those listed in the first part of the flexible overhead budget. Both price and quantity differences can cause spending variances for these items. The actual price paid for an item may differ from the expected price used in establishing the flexible budget. For example, oil is budgeted at $1.00 per quart but the actual price paid is $1.40; an unfavorable price variance will result.

On the other hand, the actual quantity used of an input may differ from the estimated quantity. For example, the budget might call for 10 gallons of oil per 1,000 units produced. If 11 gallons per 1,000 units are consumed, an unfavorable volume variance will result.

As we saw with direct materials and direct labor variances, managers must decide whether a controllable variance is large enough to warrant investigation. Managers often use percentages of the budgeted amount, absolute dollars, or some combination of those measures to help them decide what to investigate. If an investigation is needed, a performance report serves as the starting point.

The responsibility for allocated costs, such as maintenance, has to be shared by two or more managers. A manager of a machining department would be responsible for controlling the amount of maintenance service used in that department. But the manager of the maintenance department is responsible for the cost of providing that service. The manager of the machining department can minimize the quantity of maintenance required by seeing that workers use machinery carefully. But the manager of the maintenance department is responsible for seeing that the work is done as carefully and efficiently as possible.

Other allocated costs are not necessarily controllable by department managers. Part of the cost of maintaining a company cafeteria, for example, might be allocated to the machining department based on the number of workers in that department.

But the manager of the machining department can do nothing to control the number of workers in the department who eat in the cafeteria. Since these allocated costs are not controllable by the machining department manager, a strong argument can be made for not allocating such costs to the department on the basis of use. However, because these costs are included in the price of products and because managers should be reminded of all costs associated with a business, these costs are often allocated.

Whether or not these noncontrollable costs are allocated, flexible budgets and performance reports should be prepared for service departments. In this way actual costs for service departments can be compared with estimated costs for the departments' activity levels. The key to implementing a flexible budget in a service department is to identify some measure of output responsible for fluctuations in such costs. Some commonly used output measures are given below:

Manufacturing Service	Output Measure
Repairs and maintenance	Repair hours
Cafeteria	Number of employees served
Power plant	Kilowatt-hours generated
Materials handling	Pounds of material moved
Production scheduling	Number of orders processed
Personnel	Number of employees served

APPLICATION OF FLEXIBLE BUDGETS TO NONMANUFACTURING ACTIVITIES

Although flexible budgets have been used to plan and control manufacturing overhead costs for years, managers have only recently begun to rely on them to control nonmanufacturing activities. Given the fact that the United States is moving more to a service economy, this is particularly important. This extended use is logical, however, since flexible budgets can be developed for any repetitive activity producing a measurable output, including selling and administrative functions.

The first step in establishing a flexible budget for a nonmanufacturing activity is to decide how the activity's output will be measured. The criterion for selecting an activity measure is the same as that used in manufacturing departments. That is, you should select the activity measure most closely related to fluctuations in the activity costs. Some typical nonmanufacturing activities and their related output measures are shown in the following list:

Activity	Output Measure
Warehousing operations	Pounds or crates handled
Packing of finished goods	Units processed
Delivery of products	Number of miles driven
Motor pool	Number of miles driven
Order entry	Number of orders processed
Billing	Number of bills processed
Data entry	Number of forms processed

Once the appropriate activity measure is shown the usual procedures for establishing a flexible budget (previously discussed) are followed. Service department costs are classified as controllable or noncontrollable, and their fixed and variable components are identified. The accounting system records actual costs for each item and compares them with the flexible budget amounts.

The major difference between manufacturing and nonmanufacturing costs is not in budgeting procedures but in variances. There are no volume variances for nonmanufacturing activities.

CHAPTER PERSPECTIVE

In this chapter we have delved into the manner in which a budget can be adjusted as business activity changes during a business cycle such as an operating year. We have seen that standards can be set for all overhead costs for a manufacturing operation as well as most major expenses in a nonmanufacturing (service) activity. Even more important, once standards can be set, you know that, as business activity changes, you're able to determine what changes in your business results are due to budget variances (composed of spending variances and efficiency variances) as well as volume variances. Thus, to the extent that your overhead costs change because of the amount consumed or the cost paid for them, you know that you're able to identify the manner in which they impact results of the company (or a division of the company) during the time they were engaged in those activities.

You have also had an opportunity of seeing how favorable and unfavorable variances can be analyzed to determine where corrective action needs to be taken for your business on a going-forward basis. It is not essential that the average business person become an expert in the detailed mechanisms of how variances are created. It is more important that a company have some type of accounting system in place. Owners and managers must reserve their time for the important analysis of the variances so that they can take corrective actions. To put it another way, managers should be doctors, not lab technicians—people who can diagnose problems as opposed to people who collect the information for the diagnostician.

Now that we have delved into the most detailed areas of cost analysis, it is important to see how these concepts are used not merely for controlling costs, but also for controlling revenues and profits of the company. For this we move to Chapter 18.

Performance Measurement: Revenue and Profit Centers

18

INTRODUCTION AND MAIN POINTS

In this chapter we will develop your understanding of the measurement of performance of people who are responsible for revenues in businesses and divisions of businesses as well as the bottom line (i.e., net profits). Up to this point we have identified mostly with the control of costs and the evaluation of performance of people who are responsible just for cost containment. In this chapter we shall broaden the focus to include people who have wider responsibilities in the company.

After reading the material in this chapter:

━━You will know what a revenue center is, and who is responsible for its activities.

━━You will understand how to compute variances for a revenue center in order to better control the behavior of that activity.

━━You will have an introduction to the concept of sales mix as an important element in determining how the revenues of a business are progressing and how the change in the sales of products in that business can impact revenues.

━━You will understand the ways of computing revenue and expense variances for a profit center.

━━You will have an appreciation for performance analysis of profit centers located in different territories, distribution channels, and product lines.

Up to now we have seen that a business manager's financial responsibility is defined by the type of responsibility center he or she manages. Each type of center involves different managerial responsibilities which calls for different reporting practices. Reporting systems for expense center managers have been covered in prior chapters. This chapter discusses reporting systems for managers of revenue and profit centers.

REVENUE CENTERS

Managers of revenue centers are responsible for achieving budget levels of contribution margin. They do so by selling budgeted quantities of various products at budgeted prices. Managers of revenue centers attempt to control the number of units sold, the product mix, and selling prices in order to achieve their contribution margin.

Selling the budgeted numbers of units is important to achieving an organization's net earnings goal. If a record store plans to sell 150,000 units per year, achieving its target profit would be difficult to meet if actual sales are only 120,000.

The product mix, or relative proportion in which various products are sold, is equally important. Suppose that our record store plans to sell 45,000 CDs and 105,000 albums? This sales plan calls for a mix of 30 percent CDs and 70 percent albums. Achieving this planned sales mix is important. Suppose the selling price and profitability are higher for CDs than for albums. Even though the store met its 150,000 units sales goal by selling 30,000 CDs and 120,000 albums, this sales mix makes it impossible to meet the contribution margin goal.

The record store must also sell products close to their budgeted selling prices. Suppose the plan is to sell CDs at an average price of $18. If the store achieves its planned sales of 45,000 CDs by selling them at an average price of $16 each, sales revenues at year end will fall short of budgeted sales revenue. Of course, not every CD must be sold at $18 to meet the sales price goal. Some CDs will be sold at more than $18, others will be discounted. As long as an average selling price is $18, the sales price goal will be met.

In seeking to achieve the budgeted average selling price, a revenue center manager may shift emphasis from one product to another. For example, a store manager may decide to emphasize classical CDs, whose average selling price is relatively high in order to achieve the budgeted average selling price. Thus, revenue center managers trade off sales of one product for another in trying to achieve their revenue goals. If budgeted quantities of products can be sold at the planned average selling price, such trades will be successful and managers will achieve their total revenue goals.

Variance analysis is equally important in this area. Three types of variances are used to measure revenue center managers in meeting their goals:

1. Sales price variance
2. Sales volume variance
3. Sales mix variance

As an example of how revenue variances can be useful, suppose that the Kelly Division of ABC Corporation has budgeted revenues of $80,000. At the end of the month accountants report actual sales of $88,000. The division manager is pleased, but what caused sales to go over budget? Was some new sales strategy particularly successful? Or was the cause some other factor within the manager's control?

Revenue variances can help managers identify possible causes of differences between budgeted and actual sales. Assume that Kelly's budget was based on the expectation that 160,000 units of a product would be sold for $.50 each. The product would then yield revenues of $80,000. The $8,000 increase over planned revenue may have been caused by (1) a 10 percent increase in unit sales, (2) a $.05 increase in selling price, or (3) some combination of changes in sales volume and price.

Knowing sales volume and sales price variances helps business people identify the cause of any differences between budgeted and actual revenues. With that information managers will be better positioned to decide what action, if any, to take. In this case, if the increased revenue arose from both higher unit sales and a higher selling price, the combination should be continued and, if possible, applied to the business's other products. If the variance resulted from higher unit sales and a lower selling price, the manager may try maintaining the number of units sold while increasing the selling price.

Revenue variances are also useful in evaluating product mix. Product mix is an issue when a revenue center sells more than one product, as most do. As we have seen, the mix of products sold is important, since products usually have different contribution margins. An organization can achieve its total revenue goals but not its contribution margin goals if the product mix differs from the budgeted mix.

To get a feeling for this look at the figures for Tristan Services, on the next page.

TRISTAN SERVICES BUDGETED AND
ACTUAL HOURS BILLED,
REVENUE, AND CONTRIBUTION MARGIN FOR
THE MONTH OF OCTOBER, 1989

	BUDGET			ACTUAL		
	Word-processing	Book-keeping	Totals	Word-processing	Book-keeping	Totals
Hours	250	100	350	280	84	364
Revenue	$2,000	$1,500	$3,500	$2,240	$1,260	$3,500
Contribution margin	$ 500	$ 700	$1,250	$ 560	$ 630	$1,190

CALCULATION OF REVENUE VARIANCES

The extensive coverage of variances in the manufacturing area in Chapter 16 and 17 should have given you a feel for how variances are computed and utilized. Now, at this point, let us just survey the elements that make up the variances for a revenue center.

Sales Price Variance

A change in a sales price will change total revenue, contribution margin, and earnings. The contribution margin must change because, by definition, it is determined by the sales price as follows:

Contribution margin per unit *equals* Sales price per unit *minus* Variable expenses per unit.

This sales price variance shows how much of the difference between actual and budgeted contribution margin is caused by a difference between actual and budgeted sales prices.

Sales Volume Variance

The sales volume variance is a measure of the difference between actual unit sales and budgeted unit sales. The best measure of how a change in the sales volume will affect profitability is also the change in contribution margin. The accountant multiplies the difference between actual unit sales and master budget unit sales (as explained in Chapter 13) by the master budget average contribution margin per unit. In turn, the master budget average contribution margin per unit is computed by dividing the total contribution margin as stated in the master budget by the total units budgeted to be sold in the master budget. The formula is, therefore, as follows:

Sales volume variance = (Actual unit sales − Master budget unit sales) × Master budget average contribution margin per unit.

Sales Mix Variance

The sales mix variance is a measure of the change in contribution margin caused by selling products in proportions different from those that were budgeted. It is calculated by using a flexible budget. Recall that as sales volume changes, total revenue and total variable expenses are expected to change in direct proportion to volume, whereas total fixed expenses remain constant. This is the basic assumption behind the flexible budget, which shows what total revenue and total variable expenses should have been for the actual sales volume.

A sales mix variance is calculated in four steps:
1. Calculate a flexible budget for actual sales budget volume.
2. Calculate the flexible budget average contribution margin per unit by dividing the flexible budget total contribution by the actual volume of units sold.
3. Calculate the master budget average contribution margin per unit by dividing the master budget total contribution margin by the total budgeted volume.
4. Subtract the master budget average contribution margin per unit (obtained in Step 3) from the figure computed in Step 2.

By following these steps we will be able to determine whether the sales mix variance is favorable or unfavorable. Where the flexible budget average contribution margin per unit is *less* than the master budget average contribution margin per unit, the variance will be unfavorable. It would be favorable if the flexible budget average contribution margin per unit were *greater* than the master budget average contribution margin per unit.

CALCULATION OF EXPENSES AND REVENUE VARIANCES FOR PROFIT CENTER MANAGERS

Having considered the revenue center element, let us now take a look at a profit center. Because managers of profit centers are responsible for both revenues and expenses (i.e., the "bottom line"), they are interested in evaluating both revenue and expense variances. Usually profit center managers do not want detailed standard reports and flexible budget expense variance reports. These reports are useful to managers of expense centers, who report to profit center managers. Profit center managers need only a summary of how expenses are being controlled. Expense and revenue variances are generally calculated for the center as a whole using the following type of master budget, flexible budget, and actual sales information shown in the Stoner Company report.

STONER COMPANY
MASTER BUDGET, FLEXIBLE BUDGET,
AND ACTUAL RESULTS
FOR THE MONTH OF MAY, 1989

	Master Budget	Flexible Budget	Actual
Sales in units	10,000	10,100	10,100
Sales revenue	$115,000	$115,400	$113,000
Variable expenses			
Manufacturing	$ 40,000	$ 39,900	$ 37,300
Marketing	22,500	22,850	25,765
Total variable expenses	$ 62,500	$ 62,750	$ 63,065
Contribution margin	$ 52,500	$ 52,650	$ 49,935
Fixed expenses			
Manufacturing	$ 18,000	$ 18,000	$ 18,130
Marketing	14,000	14,000	14,280
Administration	8,000	8,000	7,950
Total fixed expenses	$ 40,000	$ 40,000	$ 40,360
Operating income	$ 12,500	$ 12,650	$ 9,575

Notice that Stoner's actual variable marketing expenses were $25,765, whereas the master budget allowed only $22,500. This discrepancy does not necessarily represent an expense control problem. Remember that the actual sales volume was 100 units higher than planned. When actual volume is above budgeted volume, variable expenses are expected to increase. The question is whether variable marketing expenses increased more or less than expected. The answer is in the flexible budget, which shows the level of variable expenses the company should expect for the product mix anticipated. According to the flexible budget, variable marketing expenses might be expected to increase to $22,850. If so, part of the $3,265 increase in marketing expenses is justified by the increased sales volume. An expense variance quantifies that part of the expense increase that volume increases cannot justify.

Once the master budget, flexible budget, and actual sales and expense data are compared, we can calculate the variances needed by the profit center manager. Remember that the goal of the profit center manager is to ensure that actual earnings equal or exceed master budget earnings. There are four basic reasons that master budget earnings and actual earnings might differ:

1. Actual sales volume differs from master budget sales volume; this causes differences in revenue, variable expenses, contribution margin, and earnings.

2. Actual sales mix differs from the master budget sales mix; this causes differences in revenue, variable expenses, contribution margin, and earnings.

3. Actual sales price per unit differs from the master budget sales price per unit; this causes differences in revenue, contribution margin, and earnings.

4. Actual expenses differ from flexible budget expenses; this can cause differences in total variable expenses, contribution margin, total fixed expenses, and earnings.

By carefully comparing master budget, flexible budget, and actual sales and expense data, the profit center manager can determine which of these four might be responsible for an increase or decrease in the center's earnings.

By looking at the Stoner Company report on the next page, we can see how all these items come together. Department managers are not interested in the combined variances shown at the bottom of the last two columns. They are usually interested in the line-by-line breakdowns. Variances in volume and mix are shown in the next-to-last column. They are found by subtracting figures in the master budget column from corresponding figures in the flexible budget column. These variances reflect differences in volume and mix only.

Price and expense variances are shown in the last column. They are found by subtracting each figure in the flexible budget column from the corresponding figure in the actual column. Since both the actual column and the flexible budget column are based on actual sales volume and mix, differences between the two columns must be caused by differences between actual sales prices or expenses and those estimated.

A profit center manager using this report would probably start at the bottom. He or she would observe that actual earnings were significantly below master budget earnings. Then the manager would check the right-hand column, which shows three

STONER COMPANY
VOLUME AND MIX VARIANCES AND
EXPENSE AND PRICE VARIANCES
FOR THE MONTH OF MAY, 1989

	Master Budget (a)	Flexible Budget (b)	Actual (c)	VARIANCES Volume and Mix (b−a)	VARIANCES Price and Expense (c−b)
Sales in units . . .	10,000	10,000	10,100	100(F)	
Sales revenue . . .	$115,000	$115,400	$113,000	$400(F)	$2,400(U)
Variable expenses					
Manufacturing	$ 40,000	$ 39,900	$ 37,300	$100(F)	$2,600(F)
Marketing . . .	22,500	22,850	25,765	350(U)	2,915(U)
Total variable expenses	$ 62,500	$ 62,750	$ 63,065	$250(U)	$ 315(U)
Contribution margin	$ 52,500	$ 52,650	$ 49,935	$150(F)	$2,715(U)
Fixed expenses					
Manufacturing	$ 18,000	$ 18,000	$ 18,130	$ 0	$ 130(U)
Marketing . . .	14,000	14,000	14,280	0	280(U)
Administration	8,000	8,000	7,950	0	50(F)
Total fixed expenses	$ 40,000	$ 40,000	$ 40,360	$ 0	$ 360(U)
Operating	$ 12,500	$ 12,650	$ 9,575	$150(F)	$3,075(U)

FOOTNOTES

(F) *Favorable*

(U) *Unfavorable*

large variances: (1) a $2,400 unfavorable variance in the sales price; (2) a $2,600 favorable variance in variable manufacturing expenses; and (3) a $2,915 unfavorable variance in variable marketing expenses.

Next, the profit center manager would ask a revenue center manager to explain the cause of the $2,400 sales price variance. A marketing manager would need to investigate the $2,915 unfavorable variance in the variable marketing expenses. Similarly, the expense center manager should investigate the $2,600 favorable variance in variable manufacturing expenses. Perhaps the cause of this last variance can be applied elsewhere to produce similar favorable results. Because the variances in fixed expenses are 2 percent or less of the budgeted amounts, the profit center manager would probably decide they are too small to investigate.

The combined sales mix and sales volume show only in a net $150 favorable variance. The profit center manager might ask the revenue center to divide the variable variance into its two components and take a look at which of the two gives a further clue as to whether there is a netting effect that results in the small variance.

PERFORMANCE ANALYSIS BY SALES TERRITORY, DISTRIBUTION CHANNEL, AND PRODUCT LINE

We learned earlier that businesses are generally organized in one of three major ways: by function, by geography, or by product line. Up to this point we've been looking at performance measurement in a functionally organized company. This is a company in which one manager is responsible for manufacturing, one manager for marketing, and so on. This type of structure is found mostly in small- and medium-size companies with only one revenue center and one profit center. In companies organized by geographic territory or product line, accountants must calculate these variances separately for each area or product. Even in functionally organized companies, variances might be reported by territory, distribution channel, or product line to obtain a more precise indication of the source of a variance.

It is beyond the scope of this book to delve into those subjects in detail. The principles that we have discussed are similar, and the reader now has the tools to look into those subjects by territory, distribution channel, or product line if the company is a more complicated one. A few words of explanation might be beneficial in that regard.

Analysis By Territory

Functionally organized companies are often subdivided by geographic sales territories. That is, the marketing manager has overall responsibility for sales, but responsibility for sales in a particular region is delegated to a district manager. In such cases each district manager is a revenue center manager.

The revenue center manager is not concerned with manufacturing or administrative expense variances. Only those variable marketing expenses incurred directly in the territory are deducted from the territory contribution margin. Instead of showing earnings, the bottom line of the revenue center report will show a territory's contribution to overall profitability.

Analysis by Distribution Channel

A national department store chain might have a manager for each market region as well as each distribution channel. For example, catalog sales or retail sales are probably managed separately, even if they are both housed in the same building. This is because each department requires specialized expertise. Naturally, each manager would want to see variance pertaining exclusively to his or her distribution channel.

Or suppose a single manager is responsible for wholesale, mail order, and telephone sales. If the department experiences a large sales volume variance, the first thing the manager would want to know is which channel produced the discrepancy. Thus, if the variance occurred mainly in the telephone sales, the manager could direct his attention toward that distribution channel and waste no time on the others.

To meet the needs of this manager, accountants would prepare variance reports similar to the ones we've seen earlier. A difference would be that figures are reported by distribution channel rather than territory. The manager could then tell not only the channel to which a variance pertains but whether the problem was one of sales volume, price, or mix.

Analysis by Product

Revenue center managers are often responsible for more than one product. In such cases, they may require a separate variance report for each product. This type of analysis is similar to reports on territories and distribution channels, except that there is no sales mix variance. The following small company report gives the Western region manager further information on the region's performance.

There is a $7,000 favorable sales volume variance for Product Red. If total sales volume and mix variances for the territory was less than $7,000 favorable, the total favorable sales volume variance must be caused by sales for Product Red.

The manager can also tell that the unfavorable sales price variance resulted directly from Product Red without even calculating the price variances for other products if the total unfavorable variance was about $9,750.

SMALL COMPANY, WESTERN REGION
CONTROL REPORT FOR PRODUCT RED
FOR THE YEAR ENDED DECEMBER 31, 1989

	Master Budget (a)	Flexible Budget (b)	Actual (c)	VARIANCES Sales Volume (b−a)	VARIANCES Price and Expense (c−b)
Sales in units	60,000	65,000	65,000	5,000	
Sales revenue . . .	$90,000	$97,500	$87,750	$7,000(F)	$9,750(U)
Variable expenses					
Manufacturing	$38,400	$41,600	$41,600	$3,200	$ —
Marketing	9,000	9,750	9,100	750(U)	650(F)
Total variable expenses	$47,400	$51,350	$50,700	$3,950	$ 650
Contribution margin	$42,000	$46,150	$37,050	$3,550(F)	$9,100(U)

FOOTNOTES

(F) *Favorable*

(U) *Unfavorable*

The manager could note the favorable variance for variable marketing expenses. This variance means that the Western region spent less than the flexible budget allowed for Product Red, given the actual sales volume.

The overall variance in Product Red contribution margin was an unfavorable $9,100. The contribution margin lost from a lower sales price was greater than the contribution margin gained from increased sales volume and reduced variable marketing expenses. The manager of the Western region must ask whether there is some way of maintaining Product Red sales volume at the budgeted price. If so, the favorable sales volume variance would bring a higher profit to the company.

CHAPTER PERSPECTIVE

In this chapter you have seen how performance measurement is expanded to people responsible for revenues as well as profits in the company. We have expanded on earlier discussions, which focused solely on measurement in terms of control of costs. At this point in time you have an understanding of the way in which variances in revenues and variances in profit can be analyzed for more effective management of your business. You also have an understanding of how this can be done in terms of people responsible for certain sales territories, certain parts of your distribution channel, as well as people responsible for one or more product lines. At this stage, therefore, we are at a point of looking at the role of performance management as it will be exercised by the most senior people in a business, namely, those responsible for investment centers.

Performance Measurement: Investment Centers

INTRODUCTION AND MAIN POINTS

In this chapter we will round out our discussion of performance management by looking at those people who are responsible for the proper management of the investments made in certain parts of a business or by the company as a whole. These would be the most senior executives of your company.

After studying the material in this chapter:

━ You will have a fundamental understanding of how a return on investment (ROI) is calculated, and the significance of it to the bigger picture in the measurement of the activities of the company as a whole or of a segment of the company.

━ You will see how the return on investment can be separated into a number of components so that individual portions in the formula can be utilized as a performance measurement standard.

━ You will have a feeling for the manner in which earnings are computed for investment (or profit) centers with particular emphasis being put on the manner in which costs of the company are allocated to such centers.

━ You will have an appreciation for the role that transfer pricing plays in the movement of goods and services between various portions of the company and how those transfer prices impact the measurement of the various centers of the company.

━ You will know the way in which investment is computed for various segments of a company, which is important in the computation of return on investment.

In Chapter 18 we saw that a responsibility accounting system provides information tailored toward various managers' responsibilities. Low-level managers generally receive detailed reports, whereas higher-level managers receive summary reports. We have also studied reporting for three of the four main types of financial responsibility centers: expense centers, revenue centers, and profit centers. We'll now look at reporting guidelines for the highest level of responsibility, namely an investment center.

To put investment center reporting into context, we will briefly review the financial responsibility of expense, revenue, and profit center managers. An expense center manager is responsible for completing assigned tasks within budgeted or standard cost levels. A revenue center manager, on the other hand, is responsible for selling budgeted quantities of various products or services at budgeted prices in order to earn the budgeted contribution margin. Revenue center managers need also to be responsible for controlling some marketing expenses. Finally, a profit center manager is responsible for achieving budgeted earnings. Thus, this manager's responsibilities are broader than those of either an expense or a revenue center manager, since he or she controls *both* expenses and revenues.

An investment center manager has even broader responsibilities, balancing revenue, expenses, and investments to achieve a budgeted return on investment. Owner-operators and heads of divisions of companies are investment center managers. These managers have substantial authority in deciding whether or not to develop, produce, and market products or services.

Their decisions may require added investment as well as leading to added revenue and expenses. To help investment center managers gauge their progress toward meeting their financial goals, accountants use various measures. The most common is return on investment (ROI), calculated as shown below:

$$\text{Return on Investment} = \frac{\text{Center's earnings}}{\text{Center's average investment}}$$

Notice the use of the word *center*, as in center's earnings, center's investment. The distinction between the profit and investment of an investment center and that of a *total* organization is important. There are some problems in determining the profit and investment of a part of an organization. We will look at them shortly. For now, however, remember that to be a useful measure of performance, ROI must be calculated by using the proper values for earnings and investment. In addition, managers must have control over their center's revenue, expenses, and investment.

HOW DO YOU CALCULATE ROI?

The Smags Theater will be used to illustrate how ROI is calculated. The theater, which is part of a theater chain, earned $60,000 last year. The investment in the theater was $400,000. Thus, Smags Theater's ROI was 15 percent.

By itself, Smags Theater's ROI is not very informative. To be useful it must be compared with the budgeted ROI.

Companies using ROI to evaluate the performance of investment center managers generally set budgets a year in advance. When a year's results are in, actual ROI is compared with budgeted ROI. Had the budgeted ROI been 12 percent for the Smags Theater, the center's financial performance would have been judged good. Had the target ROI been 20 percent, the 15 percent ROI could have reflected poor performance by the manager.

While it can be computed in many ways, budgeted ROI is usually based on three considerations:

1. The budget for the coming year, which shows:
   a. expected earnings under expected market conditions
   b. capital available to the center
2. The average ROI recently earned by competitors
3. The ROI earned by the investment center in past years

THE DUPONT FORMULA

The manager of an investment center usually receives reports that include an income statement, a balance sheet, and such selected statistics as the center's ROI. If actual ROI is below budget ROI, the manager must find out why financial performance is below expectations, so performances can be improved. A method called the Dupont Formula breaks ROI into two separate ratios, return on sales and asset turnover.

Return on sales is the ratio of profits to total sales revenue. It is expressed as a percentage and is calculated as follows:

$$\text{Return on sales} = \frac{\text{Center's earnings}}{\text{Center's total sales}}$$

Returning to the example of the Smags Theater, suppose it had total revenue of $760,000 (its net earnings were $60,000). Its return on sales would be 7.89 percent, calculated as follows:

$$\text{Return on sales} = \frac{\$\,60,000}{\$760,000} = 7.89\%$$

Asset turnover is the ratio of total sales to average investment calculated as follows:

$$\text{Asset turnover} = \frac{\$760,000}{\$400,000} = 1.9\%$$

The Dupont Formula is important because it shows two ways to improve a manager's return on investment: (1) by increasing return on sales, and (2) by increasing asset turnover. If an investment center manager receives a report showing a below-budget ROI, then he or she should first calculate return on sales and asset turnover. If return on sales is lower than expected, the cause can then be investigated. Perhaps the average selling price was low because of unplanned discounts, or perhaps the sales mix contained more units than expected of products with a low contribution margin. If there are no problems with sales price or mix, the manager should then turn to expenses. As a start expense center managers should examine and report on their flexible budgets and standard cost variances.

If return on sales was not lower than expected, the investment center manager should examine asset turnover. First, he or she should look at sales volume as a possible cause. If total sales were within budget, the turnover for individual assets should be calculated to identify which assets are too high.

In summary, the Dupont Formula is useful because it provides the strategy for locating problems with actual ROI differences from planned ROI. Table 19-1 summarizes this strategy.

TABLE 19-1

Does Actual ROI Equal Planned ROI?

If Actual Return on Sales Differs from Planned Return on Sales:	If Actual Asset Turnover Differs from Planned Asset Turnover:
1. Is there a sales price variance?	1. Is there a sales volume variance?
2. Is there a sales mix variance?	2. Is the investment in individual assets too high?
3. Are individual expenses too high?	

PROBLEMS IN MEASURING THE EARNINGS FOR AN INVESTMENT OR PROFIT CENTER

As suggested earlier, there are some problems in calculating the profits of just one portion of a business. Actually, the same problem applies to both profit centers and investment centers.

The hardest part is deciding which, if any, corporate costs are to be allocated. Then one must also decide on the allocation method. Both of these decisions significantly affect earnings. There are many instances in companies when people responsible for investment centers will complain that they are being held responsible for numbers over which they have no control. In addition, they will argue the rationality of the method used for allocating costs. How prices are established for a business conducted between centers of the company is also a problem. These problems must all be resolved in advance, so that the way in which budgets are prepared will be consistent with how actual earnings are recorded and how performance is judged.

ALLOCATION OF CORPORATE COSTS

When accounting for an organization as a whole (without profit or investment centers), there is no need to allocate costs incurred at the corporate level. There is only one unit to which the costs may be charged. But when net earnings for various parts of an organization are calculated, one must decide what, if any, portion of corporate costs can be justly charged against the center's revenue. If costs incurred at corporate headquarters are allocated to investment or profit centers, they become an expense that reduces both budgeted and actual earnings for the center.

Without going into detail, there are two criteria for resolving such allocation problems:

1. What costs can a manager control?
2. What type of allocation will motivate a manager to make decisions in the best interest of the business?

The first criterion, controllability, was discussed when we covered controllable costs in an earlier chapter. A cost is controllable if a manager can significantly influence the amount of the cost. Control is never absolute. A manager can never completely control a cost. But if a manager can make decisions that will significantly influence cost, that cost is considered controllable.

For example, a supervisor may be unable to control employee wage rates because they are fixed annually by a union contract. However, he or she can influence employee efficiency and productivity, which controls the number of hours employees work. Thus, because the supervisor can influence a worker's productivity, labor costs are considered a controllable cost.

The second criterion, motivation, is important because one purpose of measuring performance is to encourage managers to achieve their goals. Budgeted earnings are determined in advance precisely so managers know what level of achievement is expected from them. If a manager's earnings target is $10,000 for January, and the accountants report earnings of only $8,500 at month end, that manager will be motivated to make up the $1,500 deficiency during the remaining months of the year.

Corporate administrative expenses can be divided into two categories based on how they affect a manager's motivation. The first includes the cost of the services corporate headquarters provides to investment and profit centers. Accounting, data processing, engineering, and market research all belong in this category. The second includes general administrative expenses, which benefit centers only indirectly. Salaries of the president and vice-presidents and the cost of advertising to promote corporate image belong in this second category. Other corporate costs indirectly benefitting profit and investment centers are sometimes allocated to those centers, including interest expense and income taxes.

A good argument can be made for allocating the cost in the first category. If services were not provided by corporate headquarters, the centers would have to provide those services from another source. And even though the cost of the services is not controllable, the amount of the services requested is controllable. In fact, to motivate profit and investment center managers to use corporate services carefully, a company should charge for those services internally. Managers who are charged for a service try to keep the use of that service to a minimum. A good example of this would be a publications group within a company that provides periodicals and other printed matter needed for the operations of the profit center.

Data processing services for billing customers are usually provided for an entire organization through a large central computer. Such an arrangement is sometimes more efficient than installing smaller computers in each profit or investment center to perform this task. In the early years of data processing, companies often provided the services free of charge to encourage computer usage. But as managers became familiar with the advantages of data processing, use of the service grew, as did its cost. Companies soon began charging departments for that service, and managers began weighing the cost and benefit of requesting the service. If a manager requests more service than his or her center can effectively use, that excess cost reduces the center's profits. But to the extent that data processing services further a center's operations, they add to a center's profits. Allocating the cost of service helps ensure that services are not wasted.

The second category of corporate costs, general administrative expenses, is not controllable by center managers, either in amount or in cost. When budgeted earnings or targeted ROI are set, divisions are often compared with independent companies that incur such expenses.

Some managers believe that all corporate costs should be allocated to divisions. Not only does such an arrangement make earnings more comparable to those of independent companies, it also means that managers are more highly motivated because they know what earnings would be at the centers for independent companies. Table 19-2 summarizes the allocation of corporate costs.

TABLE 19-2

Category 1: Costs of Specific Services

Allocation to encourage center managers to control the quantity of services requested. Examples of such costs are:

Accounting	Engineering
Data processing	Market research

Category 2: Other Corporate Costs

Usually not controllable by investment or profit center managers. Allocated so a center's earnings are more comparable to those of independent companies. Examples of such costs are:

Salaries of corporate officers	Interest expense
Corporate advertising	Income taxes

EFFECTS OF TRANSFER PRICING

Another problem in measuring profits for parts of an organization is accounting for products or services transferred between divisions within the company. Normally competition determines selling prices. But competition exists only when buyer and seller are free to act in their own best interest. If one part of an organization provides another with a product, the buyer and seller may not be free to act in their own best interest because of policies set by the organization. That is, the price may not be the same as that set by the competitive market.

Sales between two divisions of the same organization result in special prices called *transfer prices*. The issues involved in setting transfer prices are a subject matter all their own and are beyond the scope of this discussion.

Suffice it to say at this point, that a transfer price is a subject of interest to people at all levels of the company. First, it is in a company's interest to avoid unnecessary friction between buying and selling divisions. If a division thinks it is at a disadvantage in doing business in-house, it is unlikely to cooperate in such arrangements, even if they benefit the company as a whole. Second, the capacity of the selling division should be used to maximize the company's overall profitability. If the selling division has idle capacity, that fact should influence the transfer price. Finally, the buying division should know the true marginal cost of the product it buys. From the buying division's point of view, the full transfer price is to be the marginal cost of the item. Yet, the marginal cost of the selling division (and, therefore, the corporation as a whole) is usually lower than the transfer price.

In practice, there are two common approaches to establishing transfer prices: market-based transfer prices and cost-based transfer prices, which are either standard variable costs or standard full-absorption costs, as we discussed those terms in a prior chapter.

The market-based price is the price at which a product can be purchased or sold by independent buyers and sellers. A market-based transfer price is the outside market price of the product, possibly adjusted for savings in transportation, credit, and other costs avoided by selling to a related division. The market price, if it can be determined, is the ideal transfer price. Generally, if a market price exists for a product or service sold in-house, firms will use it as their transfer price.

In almost all cases, cost-based transfer prices are based on standard manufacturing costs. Were they based on actual costs, the selling division could pass along the cost of inefficiencies to the buying division. That would, of course, have the undesirable effect of reducing the selling division's motivation to control costs.

Cost-based transfer prices may be based on standard variable costs or at standard full costs, as noted earlier. The major advantage of basing a transfer price on a standard variable cost is that this cost is usually equivalent to the marginal cost of a product or service. Thus, the buying division knows the total marginal costs of its product and can make pricing and selling decisions accordingly.

An important disadvantage of basing transfer prices on standard variable costs is that it produces a zero contribution margin on the selling division's sales inside the company. If the selling division adds nothing to its earnings by producing and selling to inside buyers, it has no motivation to make the sale. Indeed, if the selling division has limited production capacity, it will be motivated to sell all its products or services to outside buyers.

Full-cost transfer prices permit a selling division to add to its earnings. The full-cost transfer price equals a product's variable costs plus the fixed manufacturing costs allocated to it. Since a full-cost transfer price exceeds variable costs by the amount of fixed costs, the selling division's contribution margin equals the allocated fixed costs.

As long as a division has available production capacity and no need to give up outside sales, a contribution margin equal to fixed costs is found satisfactory. But when demand is high, the outside selling price is normally greater than full costs. In that case the selling division would prefer to sell outside and earn a higher contribution margin. The problem is that the outside sales may not maximize the firm's overall contribution margin. This difficulty can be minimized by restricting the selling division from selling outside the company as long as inside needs have not been met. Of course, such a policy could create hard feelings in the selling division.

Another disadvantage of full-cost transfer price arises in the buying division. With a standard full-cost transfer price, the buying division does not know the real marginal cost of its final product. To the buying division, a transfer price always appears to be a variable cost. If the division buys one more unit, its cost increases by the amount of the transfer price. But the additional cost to the organization as a whole is likely to be just a variable cost. As a result, the profits that selling divisions made on the basis of full-cost transfer prices may not maximize profit for the entire company.

PROBLEMS IN MEASURING INVESTMENT FOR ROI COMPUTATION

To calculate ROI for an investment center, the accountant needs a measure of the amount of money invested in each center.

Recall that the formula for ROI includes the value of the center's investment. To measure a center's investment, accountants must first answer two questions:

1. What is included in the center's investment?
2. How are the included items to be measured (assigned a dollar amount)?

The same criteria for resolving allocation problems mentioned above also apply to investment measurement. These criteria are:

1. What costs can managers control?
2. What type of allocation would motivate a manager to make decisions in the best interest of the corporation?

What is Included in an Investment?

To calculate the center's investment, accountants usually start with the assets on the center's balance sheet. Often an investment center's cash is controlled in corporate headquarters, since it is more efficient to administer a single pool of cash. In such a case cash might be excluded from a center's investment because it is an uncontrollable item. But excluding cash renders the center's ROI less comparable to that of an independent firm. The compromise could be to include in both budgets and actual reports an estimate of the amount of cash the center would need were it an independent company. Including this amount in both budgets and actual reports causes no significant differences between actual and budgeted ROI and keeps the center's assets comparable to those of an independent firm.

Idle assets are sometimes also excluded from investment when calculating ROI. Suppose an investment center owns a vacant lot next to its plant. The lot is being held for future expansion. Were the lot included in the center's investment, the manager might be motivated to sell it to reduce the denominator in the ROI ratio. No earnings would be lost, and the center's ROI would increase. Excluding idle assets discourages such counterproductive behavior, which would greatly increase the cost of future expansion.

What About Liabilities?

Should some or all of the center's liabilities be subtracted from assets when calculating investments? In terms of the balance sheet, the question is whether accountants should use the total asset figure or the owner's equity (total assets minus total liabilities). Owner's equity more realistically represents the amount an organization has invested in an investment center. Nevertheless, liabilities are usually not subtracted from assets, since borrowing is commonly controlled by corporate headquarters rather than its investment managers. Further, subtracting liabilities from investment might motivate managers to incur too many liabilities (if they can).

HOW ARE INCLUDED ITEMS MEASURED?

The question of how investment items (once determined) should be measured or what dollar value should be assigned to them is a choice among several alternatives:

1. Gross book value
2. Net book value
3. Estimated current value

Gross book value and net book value are the most common choices, as these figures are easily obtained from a company's accounting records. The only difference between the two methods is that when net book value is used, the accumulated depreciation is deducted from the cost of plant and equipment. When gross book value is used, plant and equipment are valued at the original cost, and there is no reduction for depreciation. Because both methods value assets at their original costs, which may be out of date, both may distort the real value of the center's investments. The gross book value also consistently understates the center's time-adjusted rate of return, which is sometimes called the economic return on investment.

An asset's current value is the amount it can now be purchased for. This method is appealing because it represents an organization's investment in an investment center at the time the calculation is made. However, experience shows that this current value method is used in a very small percentage of firms. In this connection, it should be noted that although there are some difficulties involved in calculating an ROI when net book value is used, about 85 percent of firms prefer that method; 14% use gross book value. Consequently, these figures seem to show a strong desire by management to use the same method of valuing assets for ROI computation as is used in preparing balance sheets.

MEASURES OF PERFORMANCE

Even when its components have been properly defined, ROI should not be used as the sole criterion of divisional performance. Over-emphasis on ROI can cause an investment project whose forecast returns exceed the firm's cost of capital to be rejected merely because the project's return is less than the division's targeted ROI. This type of result can be avoided by evaluating divisional performances by various other methods, including residual income. Residual income emphasizes the added profit in dollars resulting from an investment.

Other useful performance measures include profit growth (by "profit growth" is meant the rate of increase in the net income of an investment center's activity), sales growth (by "sales growth" is meant the percentage increase in sales revenue over the operating cycle), market share (by "market share" is meant the percentage of the total sales revenue for a particular product that has been earned by the investment center being measured), working capital management (by "working capital management" is meant the extent to which the behavior of the investment center has produced improvement in the company's excess of current assets over current liabilities), new product development (by "new product development" is meant the extent to which an investment center's activities has enabled it to identify new products for the company as a whole—sometimes an important criterion since it very often happens at a time when current net income has decreased), and managerial personnel development (by "managerial personnel development" is meant the extent to which the investment center being measured has employed people whose capabilities to take on larger responsibilities has enhanced the company's future—here again, this sometimes takes place in an investment center when its net income numbers have not met targeted standards). In the long run, the net result of these items is reflected in a division's ROI, but individual examination provides a more immediate view of performance.

CHAPTER PERSPECTIVE

In this chapter we have completed our discussion of performance evaluation as it relates to the most senior level of activity in a company, namely, investment centers. This discussion has put you in a position of having a comprehensive view of the way in which company performance can be measured from the lowest levels to the highest levels of personnel. In this discussion you have seen how we turn an investment center analysis into a measurement of the ability of people running a company to monitor the activities of a company's major segments or divisions. In particular, we have seen that cost allocation to various divisions of a company is a very sensitive part of the evaluation process. In addition, we have seen that transferring products and services between divisions of a company can produce motivational advantages as well as motivational problems. And finally we have seen that the ROI calculation itself must take into account various approaches to the calculation of the investment center numbers, since they can have the result of company people taking short-range point of view in order to improve their current ROI statistics, but perhaps having detrimental effects on the company as a whole.

Index